The Attack on Pearl Harbor

Books in the Battles Series:

The Attack on Pearl Harbor
The Battle of Antietam
The Battle of Belleau Wood
The Battle of Britain
The Battle of Gettysburg
The Battle of Hastings
The Battle of Marathon
The Battle of Midway

The Battle of Stalingrad
The Battle of Waterloo
The Battle of Zama
The Charge of the Light Brigade
Defeat of the Spanish Armada
The Inchon Invasion
The Invasion of Normandy
The Tet Offensive

★ ★ ★ **Battles of World War II** ★ ★ ★

The Attack on Pearl Harbor

by Earle Rice Jr.

Lucent Books, P.O. Box 289011, San Diego, CA 92198-9011

Library of Congress Cataloging-in-Publication Data

Rice, Earle.
    The attack on Pearl Harbor / by Earle Rice Jr.
        p. cm. — (Battles of World War II)
    Includes bibliographical references and index.
    ISBN 1-56006-421-8 (alk. paper)
    1. Pearl Harbor (Hawaii), Attack on, 1941—Juvenile literature.
    I. Title. II. Series.
    D767.92.R53 1997
    940.54'26—dc20
                                                            95-35504
                                                            CIP

Contents

Foreword

Almost everyone would agree with William Tecumseh Sherman that war "is all hell." Yet the history of war, and battles in particular, is so fraught with the full spectrum of human emotion and action that it becomes a microcosm of the human experience. Soldiers' lives are condensed and crystallized in a single battle. As Francis Miller explains in his *Photographic History of the Civil War* when describing the war wounded, "It is sudden, the transition from marching bravely at morning on two sound legs, grasping your rifle in two sturdy arms, to lying at nightfall under a tree with a member forever gone."

Decisions made on the battlefield can mean the lives of thousands. A general's pique or indigestion can result in the difference between life and death. Some historians speculate, for example, that Napoleon's fateful defeat at Waterloo was due to the beginnings of stomach cancer. His stomach pain may have been the reason that the normally decisive general was sluggish and reluctant to move his troops. And what kept George McClellan from winning battles during the Civil War? Some scholars and contemporaries believe that it was simple cowardice and fear. Others argue that he felt a gut-wrenching unwillingness to engage in the war of attrition that was characteristic of that particular conflict.

Battle decisions can be magnificently brilliant and horribly costly. At the Battle of Thaspus in 47 B.C., for example, Julius Caesar, facing a numerically superior army, shrewdly ordered his troops onto a narrow strip of land bordering the sea. Just as he expected, his enemy thought he had accidentally trapped himself and divided their forces to surround his troops. By dividing their army, his enemy had given Caesar the strategic edge he needed to defeat them. Other battle orders result in disaster, as in the case of the Battle at Balaklava during the Crimean War in 1854. A British general gave the order to attack a force of withdrawing enemy Russians. But confusion in relaying the order resulted in the 670 men of the Light Brigade's charging in the wrong direction into certain death by heavy enemy cannon fire. Battles are the stuff of history on the grandest scale—their outcomes often determine whether nations are enslaved or liberated.

Moments in battles illustrate the best and worst of human character. In the feeling of terror and the us-versus-them attitude that accompanies war, the enemy can be dehumanized and treated with a contempt that is considered repellent in times of peace. At Wounded Knee, the distrust and anticipation of violence that grew between the Native Americans and American soldiers led to the senseless killing of ninety men, women, and children. And who can forget My Lai, where the deaths of old men, women, and children at the hands of American soldiers shocked an America already disillusioned with the Vietnam War. The murder of six million Jews will remain burned into the human conscience forever as the measure of man's inhumanity to man. These horrors cannot be forgotten. And yet, under the terrible conditions of battle, one can find acts of bravery, kindness, and altruism. During the Battle of Midway, the members of Torpedo Squadron 8, flying in hopelessly antiquated planes and without the benefit of air protection from fighters, tried bravely to fulfill their mission—to destroy the *Kido Butai,* the Japanese Carrier Striking Force. Without air support, the squadron was immediately set upon by Japanese fighters. Nevertheless, each bomber tried valiantly to hit his target. Each failed. Every man but one died in the effort. But by keeping the Japanese fighters busy, the squadron bought time and delayed further Japanese fighter attacks. In the aftermath of the Battle of Isandhlwana in South Africa in 1879, a force of thousands of Zulu warriors trapped a contingent of British troops in a small trading post. After repeated bloody attacks in which many died on both sides, the Zulus, their final victory certain, granted the remaining British their lives as a gesture of respect for their bravery. During World War I, American troops were so touched by the fate of French war orphans that they took up a collection to help them. During the Civil War, soldiers of the North and South would briefly forget that they were enemies and share smokes and coffee across battle lines during the endless nights. These acts seem all the more dramatic, more uplifting, because they indicate that people can continue to behave with humanity when faced with inhumanity.

Lucent Books' Battles Series highlights the vast range of the human character revealed in the ordeal of war. Dramatic narrative describes in exciting and accurate detail the commanders, soldiers, weapons, strategies, and maneuvers involved in each battle. Each volume includes a comprehensive historical context, explaining what brought the parties to war, the events leading to the battle, what factors made the battle important, and the effects it had on the larger war and later events.

The Battles Series also includes a chronology of important dates that gives students an overview, at a glance, of each battle. Sidebars create a broader context by adding enlightening details on leaders, institutions, customs, warships, weapons, and armor mentioned in the narration. Every volume contains numerous maps that allow readers to better visualize troop movements and strategies. In addition, numerous primary and secondary source quotations drawn from both past historical witnesses and modern historians are included. These quotations demonstrate to readers how and where historians derive information about past events. Finally, the volumes in the Battles Series provide a launching point for further reading and research. Each book contains a bibliography designed for student research, as well as a second bibliography that includes the works the author consulted while compiling the book.

Above all, the Battles Series helps illustrate the words of Herodotus, the fifth-century B.C. Greek historian now known as the "father of history." In the opening lines of his great chronicle of the Greek and Persian Wars, the world's first battle book, he set for himself this goal: "To preserve the memory of the past by putting on record the astonishing achievements both of our own and of other peoples; and more particularly, to show how they came into conflict."

Chronology of Events

1853
Commodore Matthew C. Perry opens Japan to Western trade.

1894–1895
Sino-Japanese War.

1904–1905
Russo-Japanese War.

1910
Japan annexes Korea.

1914
Japan enters World War I on the side of the Allies.

1921–1922
Washington Naval Conference convenes in Washington, D.C., to establish disarmament terms.

1931
Japan invades Manchuria and establishes the puppet state of Manchukuo.

1932
Rear Admiral Harry E. Yarnell conducts successful mock attack on Pearl Harbor.

1936
Japanese Navy War College publishes a *Study of Strategy and Tactics in Operations Against the United States*.

1937
Japanese troops enter China from Manchukuo and confront Chinese troops; ensuing firefight ignites full-scale war, which the Japanese refer to as the China Incident.

1939
Japan seizes Hainan Island.

1940
May Admiral Isoroku Yamamoto, commander in chief, Combined (Japanese) Fleet, starts considering a strike against the U.S. Pacific Fleet at Pearl Harbor.

June Japanese troops occupy northern Indochina.

July President Roosevelt freezes Japanese assets.

September Japan signs Tripartite Pact with Germany and Italy.

1941
January Admiral Yamamoto initiates a serious study for a surprise attack on Pearl Harbor.

March Commander Minoru Genda completes first draft of a plan to attack Pearl Harbor.

April 10 The Japanese Imperial Navy establishes the First Air Fleet (*Kido Butai*) commanded by Vice Admiral Chuichi Nagumo.

April 16 Secretary of State Cordell Hull issues Four Principles for resolving differences between the United States and Japan.

July 29 Admiral Yamamoto forms the Sixth Fleet, an advance submarine force (*Senken Butai*), under Vice Admiral Mitsumi Shimizu.

September 6 Japan decides to go to war with the United States "when necessary."

October 17 General Hideki Tojo appointed prime minister of Japan.

October 18 The Japanese general staff accepts Admiral Yamamoto's plan to attack Pearl Harbor (under threat of his resignation).

October 30 The Japanese general staff approves Proposal A, a program for continuing diplomatic dialogue with the United States.

November 3 Ambassador Joseph C. Grew warns Washington of potential surprise attack by Japan.

November 5 Admiral Yamamoto issues Operation Order Number 1, which establishes December 7, 1941, as the date of the Pearl Harbor attack (X day for Operation Hawaii). Tokyo notifies Ambassador Nomura of November 25 deadline on negotiations.

November 7 Ambassador Nomura presents Proposal A to Secretary Hull.

November 17 Officer pilots receive final briefing by Admiral Yamamoto aboard *Akagi*. Ambassador Grew again warns Washington of a possible Japanese surprise attack.

November 19 Tokyo dispatches "Winds" messages to its Washington embassy.

November 20 Nomura presents Proposal B, an alternate plan to Proposal A, to Hull; President Roosevelt prepares draft of his own modus vivendi (compromise).

November 22 Tokyo extends negotiations deadline until November 29.

November 23 Admiral Nagumo gives *Kido Butai* its operations orders.

November 24   Hull meets with representatives of Great Britain, China, Australia, and the Netherlands to discuss Roosevelt's compromise plan.

November 26   *Kido Butai* departs Etoforu for Pearl Harbor. Secretary of War Henry L. Stimson informs President Roosevelt that Japanese fleet has been sighted heading southward off Formosa.

November 27   Army Chief of Staff George C. Marshall issues War Department Message No. 472 (war warning) to Lieutenant General Walter C. Short in Pearl Harbor; CNO Admiral Harold R. Stark dispatches similar warning to Admiral Husband E. Kimmel.

December 1   Japanese leaders sign war document in Tokyo.

December 2   Admiral Yamamoto sends "Climb Mt. Niitaka" message (order to proceed with Pearl Harbor attack) to *Kido Butai*.

December 7

0600   Launching of Japanese first-wave aircraft commences.

0630   General Marshall cables second warning message to General Short (just before noon, EST).

0700   The destroyer *Ward* reports sinking of Japanese submarine.

0715   Launching of *Kido Butai*'s second-wave attackers commences.

0730   First wave arrives over northern tip of Oahu.

0749   Fuchida signals attack (*"To, To, To"*).

0753   Fuchida radios that surprise was achieved (*"Tora! Tora! Tora!"*).

0755   Attack commences simultaneously on Pearl Harbor, Fort Kamehameha, Schofield Barracks, and Ewa, Wheeler, and Hickam Fields.

0800   Admiral Kimmel cables Washington: AIR RAID ON PEARL HARBOR.

0803   *Nevada* torpedoed.

0805   *California* torpedoed twice; *Oklahoma* capsizes after being hit with five torpedoes.

0810   *Arizona* explodes.

0815   Attack on Kaneohe begins.

0825   Lieutenant Stephen G. Saltzman and Sergeant Lowell V. Klatt shoot down Japanese dive-bomber at Schofield Barracks with BARs.

0835   President Roosevelt informs Secretary Hull of Japanese attack (1405 EST).

0840   Second wave arrives over Oahu; the destroyer *Monaghan* sinks Japanese submarine.

0855   Second-wave attack begins. *Nevada* gets under way.

0900   Third attack on Ewa; *Arizona* abandoned; six SBDs from *Enterprise* arrive at Ewa.

0905   Lieutenant Mimori Suzuki crashes into seaplane tender *Curtiss*.

0907   *Nevada* struck with five bombs; the destroyer *Dale* clears harbor.

0908   *Monaghan* clears harbor.

0910   *Nevada* runs aground at Hospital Point; the destroyer *Blue* clears harbor.

0912   *Curtiss* struck again.

0920   The gunboat *Sacramento* sends rescue launch to *Oklahoma*.

0925   The cruisers *Honolulu, St. Louis, San Francisco,* and *New Orleans* bombed.

0930   Fire ignites explosions on the destroyers *Cassin, Downes,* and *Shaw.*

0945   The Japanese attack on Pearl Harbor ends.

1000   First wave arrives back at *Kido Butai*.

1030   Admiral Nagumo breaks radio silence to report to Tokyo.

1200   Commander Fuchida returns to *Akagi*.

1214   All but twenty-nine Japanese aircraft back aboard carriers.

1315   Admiral Nagumo orders withdrawal of *Kido Butai*.

December 8

1200   Shortly after noon (EST), President Franklin D. Roosevelt asks Congress to declare a state of war existing with Japan as of December 7.

Two Choices

The carriers and their escorts steamed steadily through the wintry waters of the northern Pacific. Gale-force winds and huge waves tossed them about mightily. They had crossed a large expanse of ocean on the way to their destination, forty miles northeast of Kakaku Point on the island of Oahu, and arrived on the seventh day of the month. A half hour before dawn, the carriers launched 152 airplanes for an attack on mili-

An aerial view of Pearl Harbor, with Ford Island and Battleship Row at the extreme left.

tary bases at Pearl Harbor and surrounding areas. It was a Sunday morning.

Base commanders on Oahu had been warned to expect some kind of attack. Yet when the carrier planes roared out of the rain clouds that capped the Koolau Range, they caught the Ford Island Naval Air Station, the army's Hickam and Wheeler Fields, and the Wailupe radio station by surprise. No defensive aircraft rose to meet the brazen attackers. All attackers returned safely to their carriers to complete a most successful mission. A later judgment credited the raiders with inflicting enormous destruction across the undefended island.

A Hint of Future Shock

Was this the judgment of Japan's sneak attack on Pearl Harbor on December 7, 1941? Not at all. This was the assessment of American military analysts following the Grand Joint Army and Navy (training) Exercise carried out in Hawaiian waters on February 7, 1932.

This exercise involved a major portion of the U.S. Pacific Fleet and, according to official records, was intended

> to train the two Services in the joint operation involved in the defense of such an area. More specifically it is to determine the effectiveness of the air, surface, sub-surface and land defenses of Hawaii to repel such an attack.

Rear Admiral Harry E. Yarnell, commander of the navy's attack force, shunned traditional naval strategy that relied on battleships and cruisers as offensive mainstays. In directing the mock attack on Pearl Harbor, the air-minded and forward-looking Yarnell served notice that the aircraft carrier would soon replace the battleship as the principal ship in the navies of the world.

Leaving battleships and cruisers behind, he raced across the Pacific from California with the carriers *Lexington* and *Saratoga* and a destroyer escort. Although alert to the imminence of an attack, the military installations on Oahu expected an attack more in keeping with conventional naval practices. Admiral Yarnell's carrier-based air strike at dawn caught Oahu's defenders totally by surprise and achieved great success.

This demonstration of the island's defensive unreadiness should have sounded a warning note to responsible American military leaders, but the note went unheard or at least unheeded. Naval strategists of that time believed that the presence of battleships would sharply limit carriers in their freedom of movement. The prevailing attitude, therefore, was to assign carriers to perform only an auxiliary role in naval warfare.

Rear Admiral Harry E. Yarnell (left) used the aircraft carriers Saratoga *and* Lexington *(above) to simulate an attack on Pearl Harbor in 1932. Yarnell's demonstration foreshadowed future defeats for the U.S. forces.*

Discounting the powerful performance of Yarnell's carriers, the chief umpire of the training exercise concluded:

> It is doubtful if air attacks can be launched against Oahu in the face of strong defensive aviation without subjecting carriers to the danger of material damage and consequent great losses to the attacking air force. . . . As long as our fleet exists, no enemy is likely to make such an attack as this was.

The Japanese thought otherwise. In 1936 their Navy War College published a *Study of Strategy and Tactics in Operations Against the United States*. The study stated: "In case the enemy's main fleet is berthed at Pearl Harbor, the idea should be to open hostilities by surprise attacks from the air." So began Japan's preparation for the infamous attack on Pearl Harbor that drew the United States into World War II.

Opening Japan to Western Trade

Commodore Matthew C. Perry sailed into what is now Tokyo Harbor on July 8, 1853. Matthew was the younger brother of Oliver Hazard Perry, famous for reporting "We have met the enemy and he is ours" after the Battle of Lake Erie in 1813. His party comprised four warships and 560 seamen.

The younger Perry came to Japan bearing a message from U.S. president Millard Fillmore. The message, a letter written by Daniel Webster in the form of a request, was in reality an American demand that Japan open its doors to Western trade. The letter said in part:

> Our steamships can go from California to Japan in eighteen days. . . . If your Imperial Majesty were so far to change the ancient laws as to allow free trade between the two countries, it would be extremely beneficial to both. . . . It sometimes happens in stormy weather that one of our ships is wrecked on your Imperial Majesty's shores. In all such cases we ask and expect, that our unfortunate people should be treated with kindness, and that their property should be protected, till we can send a vessel and bring them away. We are very much in earnest in this. . . . We understand there is a great abundance of coal and provisions in the empire of Japan. . . . We wish that our steamships and other vessels should be allowed to stop in Japan and supply themselves with coal, provisions and water. They will pay for them, in money, or anything else your Imperial Majesty's subjects may prefer. . . . We are very desirous of this.

Without the military means to contest President Fillmore's "gunboat diplomacy," Japan consented to the American request. The Japanese opened their ports to Western trade, and they began to build a formidable army and navy.

Commodore Matthew C. Perry (pictured) and his squadron landed in Tokyo Harbor on July 8, 1853. This show of military power forced Japan to open its doors to trade with the Western world.

Japan's New Self-Image

But how did the Japanese navy grow to such a size and strength as to allow its leaders to even consider challenging the U.S. Navy, the mightiest navy afloat in all seven seas? For the answer we must look back to July 1853, when Commodore Matthew C. Perry sailed into Edo Bay (now Tokyo Harbor) with four American warships and 560 men.

Perry carried a letter from U.S. president Millard Fillmore that requested permission for U.S. ships to call at the Japanese ports of Shimoda and Hakodate, thereby opening Japan to Western trade. The letter also asked for humane treatment for any shipwrecked American sailors. Perry returned a year later to sign the Treaty of Kanagawa with Shogun Iyeyoshi.

The ancient, isolated kingdom of Japan then became exposed to Western culture, industry, and military systems. Japan adopted a new self-image and started to dream of empire and expansion. In the brief span of eighty-eight years, Japan built, trained, and equipped an army and navy equal to those of the major European nations. Along the way to becoming a world-class power, Japan began to test her growing military strength.

Japanese Expansion

The powerful Japanese navy defeats the Chinese fleet in this depiction of the Sino-Japanese War. This victory brought Japan closer to realizing its dreams of establishing an empire.

Spurred by emerging militant leaders, Japan attacked China following a disagreement over Korea. Japan quickly defeated China in the subsequent Sino-Japanese War (1894–1895) and gained possession of Formosa (Taiwan) and the Pescadores. The victory established Japan as a major military power.

The Battle of Tsushima

When Japanese forces began to prevail in the Far East during the Russo-Japanese War, Russian czar Nicholas II sent his Baltic fleet to the Orient. The czar hoped that the additional sea power might reverse the flow of battle. It did not.

Admiral Zinovy P. Rozhdestvenski, aboard the battleship *Suvorov*, commanded the Baltic group. His fleet consisted of eight battleships, eight cruisers, nine destroyers, and about twenty smaller craft. All of the vessels were either old or aging, capable as a fleet of making only nine knots under full steam. The Russian ships reached the entrance of Tsushima Strait on May 26, 1905, over seven months after departing from their Baltic ports. Rozhdestvenski entered the strait the next day.

Within the strait that separates the Tsushima Islands from Kyushu and Honshu (the southeast part of the Korea Strait), the Japanese fleet awaited Rozhdestvenski's arrival. Commanded by Admiral Heihachiro Togo aboard the battleship *Mikasa*, the Japanese fleet consisted of four battleships, eight cruisers, twenty-one destroyers, and sixty torpedo boats.

Admiral Togo enjoyed several advantages. He was fighting in home waters. His ships were newer and faster than those of his enemy, capable of fifteen-knot speeds. And his personnel were superior to the Russians in gunnery, discipline, and leadership.

The battle commenced in early afternoon, at a range of about sixty-four hundred yards. Togo maneuvered his faster fleet masterfully. By sundown Rozhdestvenski had been wounded and three Russian battleships, including *Suvorov*, were sunk. Three more Russian ships were sunk during the night. Action continued into the following day. The remaining Russian ships fled toward Vladivostok, pursued closely by Togo's fleet.

Three Russian destroyers reached Vladivostok safely. One Russian cruiser and two destroyers made safe harbor at Manila where they were interned. All other Russian ships were sunk or captured. The Japanese lost three torpedo boats.

Russian casualties totaled ten thousand killed or wounded. Japanese losses numbered less than one thousand men.

The Battle of Tsushima Strait was hailed as the greatest naval battle since Britain's Lord Admiral Horatio Nelson defeated a combined French and Spanish fleet one hundred years earlier at Cape Trafalgar. Admiral Togo emerged from the engagement as a great and much-honored national hero.

A young Japanese ensign destined for future acclaim lost two fingers of his left hand during the battle. The ensign's name was Isoroku Yamamoto.

The Russo-Japanese War (1904–1905) erupted because of disputed claims over Korea and Manchuria. Japan again prevailed quickly. As victor, she acquired possession of the southern half of Sakhalin Island and Port Arthur. The Japanese continued their expansion and annexed Korea in 1910.

In 1914 Japan entered World War I on the side of the Allies, playing a minor role in the Pacific and occupying German ports and colonies in the Caroline, Marshall, and Marianas Islands. After the war, as a member of the League of Nations, Japan was

"Second to None"

On Sunday morning, December 7, 1941, a bulky edition of the *New York Times* carried the following front-page headlines: NAVY IS SUPERIOR TO ANY, SAYS KNOX . . . SECRETARY'S ANNUAL REPORT CITES COMMISSIONING OF 325 NEW SHIPS, 2059 PLANES. The related story, datelined Washington, December 6, reported:

> The United States Navy, now in the midst of a record expansion program and recently placed on a war footing with full personnel manning the ships of three fleets, has at this time no superior in the world, Secretary [Frank] Knox stated tonight in rendering the annual report of the Navy Department.

> "I am proud to report," Secretary Knox wrote, "that the American people may feel fully confident in their Navy. In my opinion, the loyalty, morale and technical ability of the personnel are without superior. On any comparable basis, the United States Navy is second to none."

> But he cautioned that "the international situation is such that we must arm as rapidly as possible to meet our naval defense requirements simultaneously in both oceans against any possible combination of powers concerting action against us."

awarded mandate over the Caroline and Marshall Islands, and the Marianas, except for Guam (ceded to the United States by Spain in 1898).

At the 1921-1922 Washington Naval (disarmament) Conference, Japan agreed under pressure to limit her capital ship tonnage to three tons to every five tons built by Great Britain and the United States. The Washington Treaty defined a capital ship as a warship (other than an aircraft carrier) with a standard displacement of over ten thousand tons and carrying a gun with a caliber over eight inches. Many Japanese took this to mean that the Western nations would never concede equal status to their nation. Two years later, the United States affronted them again by passing an immigration act barring Japanese and certain other nationalities. The Japanese now looked upon the United States as the chief obstacle to fulfilling their dreams of building an empire, and anti-Western feelings intensified.

A Master Plan

Japan started to devise a master plan that would enable her to dominate Southeast Asia and the western half of the Pacific. The plan's success required the removal of all Western influence from this area, known to the Japanese as the "greater East Asia coprosperity sphere." This sphere stretched from the Kurile Islands southeast to the Marshall Islands, west to the Dutch East Indies, and in a sweeping arc to India.

After Hirohito (center) became emperor in 1926, Japan continued its expansion in the Far East, much to the dismay of the League of Nations.

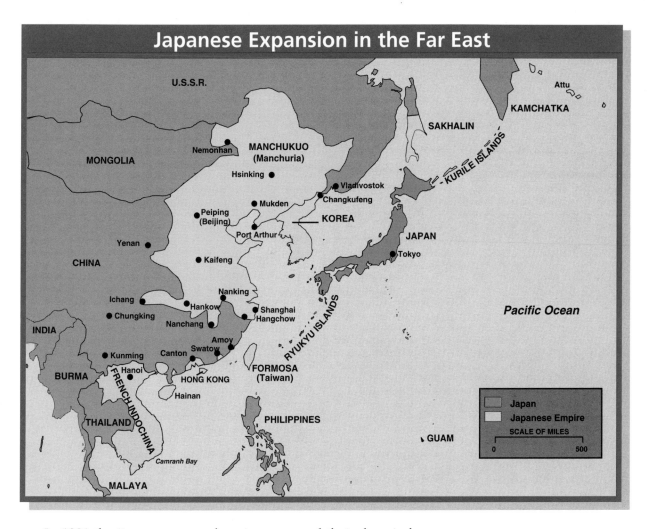

Japanese Expansion in the Far East

In 1931 the Japanese moved again to expand their domain by invading Manchuria and establishing the puppet state of Manchukuo. In July 1937, Japanese troops in Manchukuo crossed the border into China and confronted Chinese troops at the Marco Polo Bridge near Peiping (Beijing). An ensuing firefight ignited a full-scale war. Referred to as the China Incident by the Japanese, the world came to know the conflict as the Sino-Japanese War.

Japan quickly occupied a large section of eastern China, including China's capital at Peiping and most major Chinese seaports. When the League of Nations subsequently protested the Japanese aggression, Japan promptly resigned her membership.

Continuing her unrelenting advances toward the "southern resources area"—the sphere area richest in oil and other raw materials—Japan seized Hainan Island in February 1939. With the consent of Nazi-controlled Vichy France, Japan occupied northern Indochina in June 1940.

Japan next moved to show its contempt for the United States (and Great Britain, Russia, and their allies) by signing the Tripartite Pact with Germany and Italy in September 1940. The pact called for the three nations to mutually defend one another against an attack by any nation not then at war. Clearly, the only nation "not then at war" with the military strength to attack Japan was the United States.

Peace or War?

When Japan occupied all of Indochina by midsummer of 1941, the United States became gravely alarmed. President Franklin D. Roosevelt acted swiftly to curb further Japanese advances in Asia, clamping a total embargo on Japan, and freezing all Japanese assets in the United States. Japan immediately sent a team of diplomats to the United States to mediate the mounting disputes between the two countries.

Japan had to choose between two options. The first was to meet American demands to withdraw her troops from China and halt expansion in the Far East. The second option was to continue the war in China and risk war with the United States, and most likely with Great Britain and the Netherlands as well.

While diplomats in Washington discussed peaceful solutions to the Japanese-American disagreements, militarists in Japan completed their plan for a surprise attack on Pearl Harbor.

CHAPTER ONE

Operation Hawaii

If it is necessary to fight, in the first six months to a year of war against the United States and England I will run wild. But I must also tell you that if the war be prolonged for two or three years I have no confidence in our ultimate victory.

—Admiral Isoroku Yamamoto
commander in chief, Combined (Japanese) Fleet

Following the Washington Naval Conference of 1921-1922, the Japanese navy called its own conference and defined the empire's naval mission: to secure command of the western Pacific.

Japanese naval planners focused at once on what they called their "great all-out battle" strategy. This strategy was intended to lure the U.S. fleet into Japan's home waters where Japanese submarines could whittle it down to a size comparable to Japan's fleet. At some prearranged spot, the Japanese navy would then engage the American navy in an all-out battle for mastery of the Pacific.

Japan felt that this strategy would enable its navy to overcome the numerical disadvantage resulting from the shipbuilding restrictions imposed by the Washington Naval Conference. To implement this plan, Japan built a fleet designed to operate in waters close to home, with ships that emphasized speed and firepower rather than range and armor. Over the years, most high-level officials of the Japanese navy concurred in this strategy. One major figure did not agree: Admiral Isoroku Yamamoto.

The Reluctant Admiral

Yamamoto, commander in chief of the Combined (Japanese) Fleet, had been considering a strike against the U.S. Pacific Fleet at Pearl Harbor since May 1940. Having attended Harvard and served as naval attaché in Washington, D.C., in the 1920s, he had grown to like Americans and had gained great respect for America's industrial potential. Reluctant to chart a collision course with a nation potentially much stronger than his own, Yamamoto now opposed a war with the United States. Moreover, he questioned the wisdom and motives of Japan's political leaders. His reluctance should never be mistaken for fear, however, for Yamamoto was first, last, and always a patriot of unsurpassed courage.

On December 10, 1940, Yamamoto frankly voiced his growing bitterness in a letter to Vice Admiral Shigetaro Shimada, a former classmate at the naval academy:

> The present government seems to be in complete confusion. Its action in showing surprise now at America's economic pressure and fuming and complaining against it reminds me of the aimless action of a schoolboy which has no more consistent motive than the immediate need or whim of the moment. . . . It would be extremely dangerous for the [Japanese] Navy to make any move in the belief that such men as Prince Konoye and Foreign Minister Matsuoka can be relied upon.

Nor did Yamamoto believe for a minute that negotiations could resolve Japanese-American differences:

> Nomura [one of Japan's negotiators] has no confidence that he will succeed in his mission, and besides, it is expecting too much to adjust our relations with America through diplomacy at this late stage.
>
> If . . . it is felt that war cannot be avoided, it would be best to decide on war with America from the beginning and to begin by taking the Philippines, thereby reducing the line of operations and assuring the sound execution of operations. . . . The southern operations, unlike the operations in China, will

Admiral Isoroku Yamamoto, commander in chief of Japan's Combined Fleet, voiced opposition to engaging in war against the United States.

determine the nation's rise or fall, for they will lead to a war in which the nation's very fate will be at stake.

Despite Yamamoto's reluctance to fight the Americans, no one could doubt that he would serve his country well if war broke out.

The Significance of Taranto

In January 1941, as war with the West moved closer to becoming a reality, Yamamoto secretly initiated a serious study for a surprise attack on Pearl Harbor. To assist in the study of what he termed Operation Hawaii, Yamamoto called upon his chief of staff, Rear Admiral Shigeru Fukudome to find him an air officer "whose past career has not been influenced by conventional methods."

Rear Admiral Shigeru Fukudome called upon Rear Admiral Takijuri Onishi (pictured), an air officer, to assist in planning Operation Hawaii.

In strict secrecy, Fukudome recruited Rear Admiral Takijuri Onishi, then serving as chief of staff to the commander of the navy's land-based air force. Onishi faced many problems in his new assignment. One of his more important tasks was to devise a way to launch aerial torpedoes in the shallow waters of Pearl Harbor. Existing torpedoes would either bottom out in Pearl Harbor's forty-foot depths or smack the water and bounce harmlessly over the decks of intended targets.

Admiral Onishi immediately enlisted the help of Commander Minoru Genda, a brilliant young air officer recently returned from attaché duty in London. Genda accepted the task with enthusiasm.

While in London, Genda had learned about the Royal Air Force's (RAF) daring raid on the Italian fleet at Taranto on November 11, 1940. Twenty-one obsolete Fairey Swordfish torpedo bombers from the British carrier *Illustrious* had staged a night attack in the shallow (eighty-foot deep) Italian harbor. With only eleven torpedoes—modified with wooden fins—the British sank three of six Italian battleships, thereby altering the naval balance in the Mediterranean in Britain's favor.

U.S. Secretary of the Navy Frank Knox predicted that the Japanese fleet would attempt a sneak attack on Pearl Harbor.

The significance of that raid did not go unnoticed by either Genda or Yamamoto. Genda now felt certain that Japan could execute a similar successful attack against the U.S. Pacific Fleet at Pearl Harbor. The talented young aviator prepared a plan.

An Unheeded Warning

At the same time, U.S. Secretary of the Navy Frank Knox also recognized the significance of the Taranto raid. He sent a warning message to Secretary of War Henry L. Stimson, stating in part: "If war eventuates with Japan, it is believed easily possible that hostilities would be initiated by a surprise attack upon the Fleet or the Naval Base at Pearl Harbor."

Raid on Taranto

On the night of November 11–12, 1940, the British aircraft carrier *Illustrious* plowed through the Mediterranean Sea under the cover of darkness. About 170 miles southeast of Italy's heel, a dozen Fairey Swordfish lifted off the three-inch-thick steel decks of the world's first fully armored carrier.

Led by Lieutenant Commander Kenneth Williamson, the flimsy Swordfish carried mixed ordnance—six armed with torpedoes, four with bombs, and two with a split load of bombs and flares for lighting up the target area. The twelve old and frail biplanes assembled overhead and headed northwest. They were heading toward a historic rendezvous with the Italian fleet at Taranto. Another wave of nine Swordfish would follow an hour later.

The Swordfish split up at the approaches to the Italian naval base, hoping to confuse the antiaircraft gunners. Ignoring a constant barrage of protective ack-ack over the heavily defended Italian anchorage, the Swordfish plunged to the attack. Their two-wave assault left behind three Italian battleships in sinking condition, two cruisers badly damaged, and two fleet auxiliary ships sunk—about half of Italy's fleet strength. The British lost only two of their twenty-one aircraft.

The remaining ships of the Italian fleet fled from the high seas to seek safe harbor in Naples. Their flight left control of Mediterranean sea-lanes to the British at an early and critical stage of the Second World War.

At Taranto, Britain demonstrated for the first time the effectiveness of carrier-based aircraft when used as a weapon against a fleet of warships. The British success did not go unnoticed in either the United States or Japan—especially in Japan.

Stimson agreed and passed the message (which included Knox's suggestions for appropriate countermeasures) along to Admiral Husband E. Kimmel, commander in chief, Pacific Fleet (CinCPAC), at Pearl Harbor. Kimmel opposed suggestions for installing torpedo nets to protect his ships, arguing that nets would interfere with ship movements within the tight confines of the harbor. He also arrogantly rejected any suggestion that Japan might undertake a venture so far from home with her "inferior" aircraft and pilots.

Admiral James O. Richardson, commander in chief of the U.S. Fleet (CinCUS), shared Kimmel's view. He simply could not believe that the Japanese would attack American ships or their base. Neither did he feel the need to take extra precautions against an unlikely torpedo attack.

On January 7, 1941, in a memorandum to chief of naval operations (CNO) Admiral Harold R. Stark, Richardson wrote:

There does not appear to be any practicable way of placing torpedo baffles or nets within the harbor to protect ships moored therein against torpedo plane attack without greatly limiting the activities within the harbor. . . . Inasmuch as Pearl Harbor is the only operating base available to the Fleet in this area any passive defense measures that will further restrict the use of the base as such should be avoided. Considering this and the improbability of such an attack under present conditions and the unlikelihood of an enemy being able to advance carriers sufficiently near in wartime in the face of active Fleet operations, it is not considered necessary to lay such nets.

The Japanese, on the other hand, could not conceive of the Americans failing to take such precautions. They tried mightily to learn where the U.S. Navy might have installed torpedo nets in Pearl Harbor. Their efforts failed because the U.S. Navy had not installed any such nets—nets that might have spared the United States great damage to capital ships and untold casualties.

Through overconfidence in its own defensive capabilities and disbelief in a potential Japanese attack, the navy's high command failed to heed Frank Knox's clear warning.

A Risky Operation

In March 1941 Genda completed his plan for Yamamoto's Operation Hawaii. Admiral Onishi reviewed Genda's plan and gave it a 60 percent chance for success. But Onishi's superior, Admiral Fukudome, allowed the plan only a 40 percent success rating. It now became Yamamoto's turn to review Genda's proposal. He liked it.

Admiral James O. Richardson, commander in chief of the U.S. Fleet, greatly underestimated Japan's capabilities and thus failed to take precautions against a Japanese assault.

Though still opposed to a war with the United States, Yamamoto saw Operation Hawaii—a first crippling strike against the enemy—as the only assurance of Japan's success in the short run. He now took an active role in many tasks. His multiple duties included overseeing the preparation of a detailed plan, putting together the right mix of people, organizing and training fleet units, developing special ordnance (weapons and equipment), and convincing other high-level Japanese naval officers that his plan would work. The last task threatened to be the hardest of the lot.

"An Alarming Risk"

Admiral Yamamoto's plan for attacking Pearl Harbor raised many voices of dissent among members of the Japanese naval general staff. Vice Admiral Shigeru Fukudome, Yamamoto's chief of staff during the plan's conceptual stage, later became one of the plan's severest critics. Fukudome, upon promotion to chief of staff of the general staff's First Bureau in October 1941, called the plan "an alarming risk." In a meeting with Admiral Osami Nagano, chief of the naval general staff, and Nagano's vice chief, Vice Admiral Seiichi Ito, Fukudome reported his reasons for alarm:

> Not only are there all the normal difficulties inherent in such a bold operation, but there are numerous unknown factors besides. If the task force should be badly damaged and several carriers sunk, the striking power of the fleet will be decidedly weakened and the Southern Operation placed in serious jeopardy. We must ask ourselves, "Can a plan of such magnitude be kept secret?" If not, it has little chance of success, and the results will likely prove fatal. . . . Our ships' limited radius of action and the necessity for refueling at sea pose still other difficulties. Nor have we any assurance that intelligence requirements can be fulfilled. The problem there is to maintain a continuous, accurate flow of information on the exact whereabouts of the U.S. Fleet at all times. And the bulk of the Fleet will have to be in or near Pearl Harbor on the day of the attack, which is problematical.

Admirals Nagano and Ito shared Fukudome's alarm. Only after Yamamoto threatened to resign as commander in chief of the Combined Fleet did the naval general staff finally agree to his Pearl Harbor attack plan. And then, most reluctantly.

The general staff of the Imperial Japanese Navy (which held the ultimate responsibility for naval operations) did not agree with Yamamoto's plan; they said it was too risky. Their opinion gained strength when a war-games exercise held in Tokyo in August 1941 tried out the plan and showed a paper loss of two Japanese aircraft carriers.

On September 6, 1941, an Imperial Conference at last decided that Japan would go to war with the United States "when necessary." Nonetheless, arguments persisted between Yamamoto and the general staff as to how to proceed.

Some staff members favored striking south and attacking America only in self-defense, that is, only in the event that the U.S. fleet ventured westward out of Pearl Harbor. That show of U.S. sea power would surely happen, of course, given Japan's intent to take over the Philippines. In answer to Yamamoto's argument, the general staff sent him a detailed paper listing several major objections to Operation Hawaii. The staff's principal concern was the real possibility of incurring enormous Japanese casualties should the attack not be a surprise. Yamamoto, in a last-ditch effort to salvage his plan, responded dramatically to his critics.

Yamamoto's Ultimatum

On October 18, 1941, the general staff met again in Tokyo to consider war plans. Yamamoto sent Captain Kameto Kuroshima, his senior staff officer, to represent him. As Yamamoto's agent, Kuroshima faced a difficult, dual task: First, he had to obtain the staff's approval for Operation Hawaii; and second, he had to secure a firm commitment that the First Air Fleet's six carriers would be available for the Pearl Harbor attack.

Kuroshima arrived in Tokyo carrying a secret weapon to help turn aside his opposition. When Rear Admiral Sadatoshi Tomioka, the chief of the operations section of the naval general staff, renewed his opposition to Operation Hawaii, Kuroshima unleashed the secret weapon.

Admiral Yamamoto insists that his plan be adopted. . . . I am authorized to state that if it is not, then the Commander in

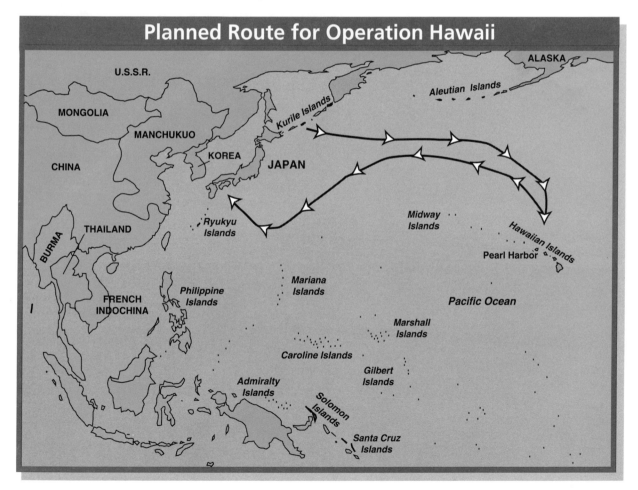

Planned Route for Operation Hawaii

Chief of the Combined Fleet [Yamamoto] can no longer be held responsible for the security of the Empire. In that case he will have no alternative but to resign, and with him his entire staff.

Kuroshima's declaration so stunned Tomioka that he took the matter to his superior, Vice Admiral Shigeru Fukudome, formerly Yamamoto's chief of staff and now chief of the naval general staff's First (operations) Bureau. Fukudome in turn elevated the matter to Vice Admiral Seiichi Ito, vice chief of the naval general staff. Ito brought the issue straight to Admiral Osami Nagano, chief of the naval general staff. Kuroshima repeated Yamamoto's ultimatum to each commander along the way and finally to Nagano. Rather than lose the services of their revered and respected commander and his loyal staff, the general staff finally yielded to Yamamoto's demands. All arguments ended.

Admiral Yamamoto threatened to resign as commander in chief of the Combined Fleet if the Japanese Imperial Navy rejected Operation Hawaii.

Japan Resolves to Go to War

In a Labor Day radio broadcast on September 1, 1941, President Franklin D. Roosevelt assured the American public that the United States possessed "a strong Navy, a Navy gaining in strength." He further declared that Americans would "do everything in [their] power to crush Hitler and his Nazi forces." President Roosevelt did not mention Japan in his speech. But the Japanese interpreted his threat against the Nazis as a threat against further Japanese expansion as well.

Two days later, Prince Fumimaro Konoye, Japan's premier, called a liaison meeting between members of the Japanese cabinet and foreign ministry to discuss the "Outline Plan for the Execution of the Empire's National Policy." After much haggling over wording, their discussion yielded a historic statement of Japanese policy. The statement declared in part:

I. Our Empire, for the purpose of self-defense and self-preservation, will complete preparations for war, with the last ten days of October as a tentative deadline, resolved to go to war with the United States, Great Britain and the Netherlands if necessary.

II. Our Empire will concurrently take all possible diplomatic measures [in relation to] the United States and Great Britain, and thereby endeavor to obtain our objectives. . . .

III. In the event that there is no prospect of our demands being met by the first ten days of October through the diplomatic negotiations mentioned above, we will immediately decide to commence hostilities against the United States, Britain and the Netherlands.

The Japanese cabinet approved this policy on September 4, 1941, as did Emperor Hirohito, two days later.

Operation Order Number One

On November 5, 1941, Yamamoto issued Operation Order Number One, which stated in part:

In the East the American fleet will be destroyed. The American lines of operation and supply lines to the Orient will be cut. Enemy forces will be intercepted and annihilated. Victories will be exploited to break the enemy's will to fight.

Yamamoto then set Sunday, December 7, 1941, as the date of the Pearl Harbor attack. The date was designated X day, the Japanese equivalent of D day (a day set for launching an operation). He selected a Sunday because he knew that Americans like to relax on weekends and that most of the U.S. fleet put into the harbor on weekends.

Operation Hawaii was on.

CHAPTER TWO

Planning and Preparation

Commander Minoru Genda used his expertise as an aviator to draft the attack plan for Operation Z in February 1941.

Although Yamamoto's proposal to attack Pearl Harbor was not approved until November 1941, advanced planning and intense preparations for Operation Hawaii—now renamed Operation Z—began in April of that year. The attack plan drafted by Commander Minoru Genda in February served as a chart to guide Yamamoto and his Combined Fleet through the rough waters that lay ahead.

Genda's Draft

Genda's draft contained eight critical elements:

1. *Surprise and absolute secrecy.* Success of the operation depended on catching U.S. forces by complete surprise. Any breach of secrecy might enable the Americans to spring a trap and inflict huge damages on the Combined Fleet. Surprise was key.

2. *American carriers as primary targets.* Genda disagreed with Yamamoto's original intent of targeting American battleships first. The air-minded commander recognized the far-ranging destructive potential of carrier-based aircraft. By eliminating American carriers without serious damage to its own carriers, the Combined Fleet would gain a huge advantage. It could then chip away at destroying the remaining U.S. fleet, free of danger from air attacks originating from American carriers. Eventually, the Imperial Navy would dominate the vast Pacific.

3. *Destruction of U.S. aircraft on Oahu.* Genda considered control of the skies over Oahu to be essential to a successful mission. He hoped to catch and destroy most of the enemy's air-

A Japanese Billy Mitchell

Historians often refer to Commander Minoru Genda as a Japanese Billy Mitchell. William "Billy" Mitchell, a visionary American army officer during the early days of aviation, is generally considered to be the father of the U.S. Air Force. It is with good reason that Genda, who was also an aviator and aerial tactician of great vision, is compared to Mitchell. Both men recognized the potential of air power and foresaw the demise of the battleship.

In mid-1936, while a student officer at the Naval War College in Tokyo, Genda proclaimed:

> The main strength of a decisive battle should be air arms, while its auxiliary should be built mostly by submarines. Cruisers and destroyers will be employed as screens of carrier groups, while battleships will be put out of commission and tied up.

Genda wrote later:

> The basic concept to support this assertion was obviously a flat denial of the hitherto long cherished concept of a sea battle . . . a concept which was built on an idea of waging once and for all a decisive gunfire engagement with battleships as the nucleus of strength. Instead, it [Genda's concept] aimed at launching a fatal series of aerial attacks upon enemy fleets from carrier groups operating a few hundred miles away from the enemy force, while land-based air forces and submarines were to support them.

craft on the ground at the beginning of the attack. Control of the air would enable his own aircraft to go about their deadly tasks unopposed. It also eliminated the possibility of an American counterstrike against the Japanese carriers.

4. *The use of all available Japanese carriers.* Shunning Yamamoto's earlier, tentative suggestion for using one, or possibly two, carrier divisions (two to four carriers), Genda insisted on using all available carriers for the attack. The military principle of mass, which entails a maximum concentration of force on an objective to yield maximum effect, guided Genda's thinking. He wanted to inflict maximum damage on the U.S. fleet. The amount of potential damage became a function of the number of available carriers. Genda eventually settled for six.

5. *The use of all types of bombing techniques—torpedo, dive, and high level—in the attack.* Although Genda favored the aerial torpedo as the most effective weapon against fleet targets, he questioned whether they could be launched successfully in Pearl Harbor's shallow waters. The possibility that U.S. ships might be protected by torpedo nets also concerned him. He opted for dive-bombing as a first alternative to a failed torpedo-bombing attack. Genda backed up his first two bombing choices by including

high-level bombing (high-altitude, level-flight approach) provisions in his draft.

6. *A strong fighter escort.* Genda foresaw a three-fold role for a strong fighter escort. Fighters would be needed to protect Japanese bombers flying to and from their targets at Pearl Harbor. These same fighters would also be required to clear the skies of enemy aircraft. A separate fighter group would be needed to form a protective umbrella over the Japanese carrier force to prevent an enemy counterattack from the air.

7. *Refueling at sea.* The limited radius of action of most Japanese ships made refueling at sea necessary. Fuel tankers would be required to accompany the attack force. Moreover, because Japanese navy personnel lacked experience in refueling at sea, they would need intensive training and practice.

8. *A daylight attack.* Japanese military aircraft of that time were not equipped with adequate instruments for conducting night operations. Accordingly, Genda specified predawn launch times so that Japanese planes would arrive over Oahu at daybreak.

A Fascinating Concept

While Genda and other aviators worked at developing the framework for an attack plan, Yamamoto's Combined Fleet staff was focusing on special tasks. The staff devoted particular attention to logistics, submarine warfare, navigation, and communications.

Yamamoto even considered the possibility of including an invasion of Hawaii as part of his attack plan. One of Yamamoto's colleagues pointed out that half the U.S. Navy was stationed in Hawaii. The capture or elimination of that many personnel would strike a crippling—even mortal—blow to American offensive capabilities in the Pacific. It was indeed a fascinating concept, and one that Yamamoto did not entirely rule out until November.

The First Air Fleet

The planning gathered momentum and moved beyond the conceptual stage, starting with major personnel and organizational changes. On April 10 the Japanese Imperial Navy established the First Air Fleet and thereby took a huge stride into the future. Traditionally, aircraft carrier divisions had been deployed as part of separate battle groups under separate command. This new organization grouped carrier divisions under a single command for the first time, a truly revolutionary development.

The First Air Fleet originally comprised two carrier divisions with two carriers each and a third division with one carrier. The First Carrier Division consisted of the carriers *Akagi*, flagship for both the division and the air fleet, and *Kaga*. Each carrier dis-

placed about 42,000 tons. *Akagi* could make thirty-one knots; *Kaga* twenty-eight. The newer carriers *Soryu* and *Hiryu* formed the Second Carrier Division. They both displaced only 30,000 tons but could attain thirty-four knots. The single, smaller and slower carrier *Ryuju* made up the Fourth Carrier Division. In addition, all three divisions included two destroyers per carrier. (The Fourth Carrier Division was used for training purposes only and did not take part in the Pearl Harbor attack.) Japan's newest carriers, *Shokaku* and *Zuikaku*, joined the First Air Fleet in September to form the Fifth Carrier Division and bring the fleet's total carrier count to six.

(Above, left) Akagi, *the flagship of the First Air Fleet. (Above) The Japanese Imperial Navy revolutionized warfare with its emphasis on aircraft carriers.*

Admiral Nagumo

To command the First Air Fleet, the navy ministry appointed Vice Admiral Chuichi Nagumo. As the housekeeping branch of the Imperial Navy, the navy ministry maintained service records and implemented promotions based on a traditional seniority system. Nagumo, with a background in battleships and cruisers, did not appear to be the most likely choice for such a command. Admiral Nishizo Tsukahara, commander in chief of the Eleventh Air Fleet and longtime friend of Nagumo's, later explained the seeming mismatch between Nagumo's experience and the requirements of his new appointment.

> Nagumo was an old-line officer, a specialist in torpedo attack and large-scale maneuvers. He was wholly unfitted by background, training, experience, and interest for a major role in Japan's naval air arm. He had no conception of the real power and potentialities of the air arm when he became Commander in Chief of the First Air Fleet.

Tsukahara's evaluation of his friend's fitness for air fleet command should be interpreted as a statement of fact rather than a criticism. It should be noted that no one in the Japanese navy rose to such high station without displaying great competence for many years in a variety of assignments. Nagumo, by any standard, had earned promotion to the lofty command.

The navy compensated for Nagumo's deficiencies as an air commander by naming Rear Admiral Ryunosuke Kusaka to serve as his chief of staff. Kusaka, although not an aviator, had previously captained the *Hosho* and *Akagi* on his climb up the ladder of naval air command.

Perhaps of greater consequence was the appointment of Commander Minoru Genda as Nagumo's air operations officer. Nagumo would come to rely heavily on the judgment and advice of the brilliant air tactician.

With the able assistance of Kusaka and Genda, Nagumo would lead his fleet through a succession of victories. It remains doubtful, however, that Nagumo ever felt really comfortable commanding an air group. He in fact strongly opposed Operation Z in the early stages of the plan. Along with the naval general staff, Nagumo believed that fleet priorities should be directed toward securing the vital oil regions in the south.

Notwithstanding his objections, however, Nagumo pitched into his new tasks with a will. He went on to compile a record of achievement unmatched by any other Japanese admiral in World War II. Whatever shortcomings and misgivings Nagumo might have displayed along the way should be measured against this record.

Rear Admiral Ryunosuke Kusaka, who had served as captain of the Hosho *and* Akagi*, was named chief of staff under Vice Admiral Nagumo.*

A Question of Attitude

Admiral Chuichi Nagumo had opposed Admiral Isoroku Yamamoto's Pearl Harbor attack plan from the beginning. Nagumo's appointment as commander of the First Air Fleet—*Kido Butai* (Striking Force)— was criticized by high-ranking Japanese naval officers. Many officers doubted the resolve of Nagumo and his fleet to execute successfully the risky operation. Rear Admiral Matome Ugaki, Yamamoto's chief of staff and one of Nagumo's strongest critics, wrote:

> What the hell is the attitude of the First Air Fleet? In view of the fact that it has evaded Yamamoto's plan from the beginning, it should have suggested others for the job since it could not control its subordinates.

> That man Nagumo—not only does he have words with others but he is given to bluffing when drunk. Even now [about five weeks before *Kido Butai*'s departure for Pearl Harbor] Nagumo is not fully prepared to send himself and his men into the jaws of death and achieve results two or three times greater than the sacrifices entailed. . . . If Nagumo and his Chief of Staff [Rear Admiral Ryunosuke Kusaka] strongly oppose this operation, and feel they cannot carry it out, they should resign their posts.

The appointment of Admiral Chuichi Nagumo as commander of the First Air Fleet caused much controversy. Many feared that Nagumo would be unable to execute the dangerous mission.

Yamamoto tended to agree with Ugaki but could find no real reason to dismiss Nagumo. In fact, Nagumo finally accepted Yamamoto's Pearl Harbor plan.

Sixth (Submarine) Fleet

Whether from lack of total confidence in Nagumo, or for some other reason, Admiral Yamamoto decided to deploy a submarine force to back up Nagumo's aviators.

On July 29 Yamamoto consulted with Vice Admiral Mitsumi Shimizu, commander of the Sixth (submarine) Fleet. Shimizu was a good-looking man of gentle nature and calm confidence, well respected by his fellow officers and the enlisted ranks. Yamamoto

Midget Submarine Crews

In his *Rengo Kantai* (Combined Fleet) Extracts, first published in April 1952 in the Japanese newspaper *Mainichi Shimbum*, Vice Admiral Ryunosuke Kusaka recalled the difficulties faced by the courageous crews of the Sixth Fleet's midget submarines:

> Among those [Sixth Fleet] submarines, five took a midget submarine each on board. It was not an easy task to make a long voyage of 3,000 miles submerging at daytime and only surfacing at night, but a more difficult task was that assigned to those young boys of the midget submarines, to whom our deepest admiration should be paid. Surely even the slightest chance of survival could hardly be seen in their assigned mission. There might be torpedo-defense nets extended along vessels, patrol boats with eagle eyes at the entrance of the bay and mine barriers laid, all of which had to be overcome to penetrate into the bay to destroy enemy vessels at one blow. When I thought of the unsophisticated spirit of those young boys, originally I thought that the spearhead of the attack would be better made by those midget submarines. But it was decided that the initial attack be made by the air forces, lest an untimely attack by midget submarines would spoil this grave operation.
>
> Topographically, the entrance of Pearl Harbor was so narrow that it was hard for a submarine with low view to observe clearly the enemy situation in the harbor. So it was arranged that the enemy situation in the harbor just prior to the attack be determined by *Tone*'s and *Chikuma*'s seaplanes, and the Lahaina anchorage, which could be searched from outside the anchorage, be scrutinized by a submarine in order to get negative information on the enemy situation. Most of those submarines left the homeland bases on or around 18 November.

approached him gravely about organizing and commanding an undersea assault force for Operation Z.

"Under present conditions I think war is unavoidable," Yamamoto began. "If it comes, I believe there would be nothing for me to do but attack Pearl Harbor at the outset, thus tipping the balance of power in our favor." Shimizu's mouth opened as if to speak, but he said nothing. Yamamoto hastened to acknowledge:

> I know the operation is a gamble, but I am absolutely convinced that it is the only method that can be used to meet the present situation. It will be the most effective way to hold the U.S. Fleet in check because this is what they will least expect.

Yamamoto paused briefly to allow the other man to recover from his surprise, then surprised him further. "I would like you to command our submarine forces as commander of the *Senken Butai* [Advance Force]."

Although he was then commander of the Sixth Fleet, Shimizu had little personal experience as a submariner. Much of his continuing surprise derived from knowing that his great commander had chosen him over many competent high-ranking veterans of submarine warfare. Shimizu's response came from the heart. "I will do my very best to fulfill your expectations."

The Big Three

The top-level leadership structure for the Pearl Harbor plan was now established and it formed an odd-shaped triangle: Yamamoto, commander in chief of the Combined Fleet, stood alone at the top, a brilliant, fearless commander who approached war with the United States with severe misgivings; Nagumo, the carrier striking force leader, a shipborne torpedo expert with no expertise in air-arm (aviation) command, anchored one point on the base; and Shimizu, the submarine fleet commander with no intimate experience with submarines, held down the other base point.

With the leadership established, preparations for Operation Z moved into high gear.

High Expectations

Admiral Shimizu formed a group of twenty-five submarines and five midget submarines to work independently of Nagumo's air fleet. Their duties in the impending operation would be reconnaissance, interception and destruction of American supply ships and warships attempting to move out of Pearl Harbor, and rescue of downed Japanese pilots. The midget subs were to slip into Pearl Harbor and torpedo any major warships that the attacking Japanese aircraft missed.

Admiral Nagumo's First Air Fleet and all its supporting units assembled in early November at Saeki Bay in Japan's Inland Sea. With Admiral Yamamoto looking on from aboard his flagship *Nagato*, the fleet conducted a full-dress rehearsal. An evaluation of the first rehearsal exercise indicated a need for improvement in several areas: Fleet rendezvous times, aircraft deployment and approaches to target, and torpedo launches all needed fine tuning. Two more rehearsals revealed continuing problems with torpedo launches, but further testing elevated the torpedo hits to an 82 percent success rate by mid-November.

On November 17, the one hundred officer pilots of the First Air Fleet (most prewar Japanese pilots were enlisted men) gathered aboard the *Akagi* for a final briefing from Admiral Yamamoto. He outlined the attack plan and appealed for their maximum effort. Yamamoto warned:

Despite his misgivings, Admiral Yamamoto inspired his fleet to proceed with the risky Operation Z.

Although we hope to achieve surprise, everyone should be prepared for terrific American resistance. . . . Japan has faced many worthy opponents in her glorious history—Mongols, Chinese, Russians—but in this operation we will meet the strongest and most resourceful opponent of all. . . . Therefore you must take into careful consideration the possibility that the attack may not be a surprise after all. You may have to fight your way in to the target.

Yamamoto ended with a reminder of their heritage and a final word of caution. "It is the custom of *Bushido* to select an equal or stronger opponent. On this score you have nothing to complain about—the American Navy is a good match for the Japanese Navy."

When Yamamoto finished his briefing, everyone retired to a farewell party held in *Akagi's* wardroom. They ate ritual fare of *surume* (dried cuttlefish) for happiness and *kachiguri* (walnuts) for victory, then toasted their emperor with *sake* (rice wine) and shouted *"Banzai! Banzai! Banzai!"* ("May you live forever!").

During the party, Yamamoto expressed confidence in the outcome of the impending attack: "I expect this operation to be a success." He expected—rather than hoped—for a success. His conviction gave heart to those about to sail into harm's way.

Instructions

On November 23 Admiral Nagumo issued a set of operations orders outlining the attack plan for members of his First Air Fleet. Briefly, the final formation of Nagumo's *Kido Butai* (Striking Force) and the operational roles assigned to individual elements of the force were as follows:

- The six carriers, *Akagi* (Red Castle, First Air Fleet flagship); *Kaga* (Increased Joy); *Hiryu* (Flying Dragon); *Soryu* (Green Dragon); *Shokaku* (Soaring Crane); and *Zuikaku* (Happy Crane), along with their 423 aircraft (353 of which were to be used in the Pearl Harbor attack), formed the nucleus and main offensive force of *Kido Butai*.

- Nine destroyers and the light cruiser *Abukuma* (escort flagship) were assigned to provide protective screening for the carriers.

- The battleships *Hiei* and *Kirishima*, with the heavy cruisers *Tone* and *Chikuma*, respectively added fourteen- and eight-inch guns as backup against unforeseen dangers. The cruisers also carried observation planes for scouting the Pearl Harbor area well in advance of the strike force.

Formation of Japan's *Kido Butai*

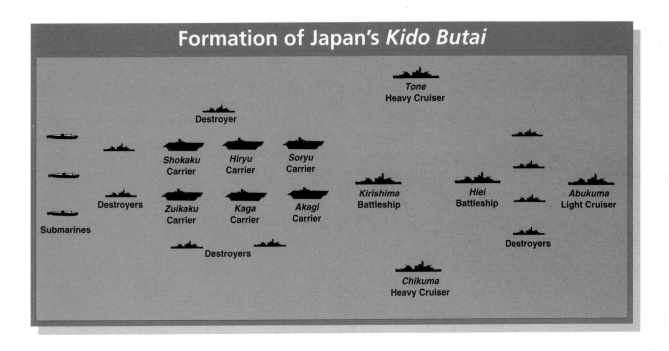

- Three submarines (not part of Shimizu's group) were designated to join *Kido Butai* at sea and patrol the waters on either side and forward of the main body on the way to Pearl Harbor.

- Seven oil tankers, slated to bring up the rear for refueling en route, rounded out Nagumo's fleet.

The fleet was to gather at Etorofu Island in the Kuriles, northeast of Japan's northern island of Hokkaido, and depart eastward, refueling as necessary. Observation aircraft were to precede the attack planes and scout out both Pearl Harbor and the alternate fleet anchorage at Lahaina Roads. The carriers would then launch their attack planes from a point about two hundred miles north of Oahu in two waves, thirty minutes apart. The attack would proceed in this fashion if all went as planned.

The first wave included all forty torpedo bombers when the opportunity for surprise would be greatest. The bombers flew low and slow, and the advantage of surprise would increase their chances of survival. Each attack element was assigned a specific target. The torpedo bombers were directed to attack carrier moorings on the northwest side of Ford Island and Battleship Row on the island's southeast side. Dive-bombers of the first wave drew targets at Wheeler Field, the army air corps fighter base, and the naval air station on Ford Island.

Dive-bombers in the second wave were assigned to targets at Kaneohe Naval Air Station, the marine airfield at Ewa, and the army bomber base at Hickam Field. Fighter planes were to escort both waves and maintain control of the air. Other second-wave

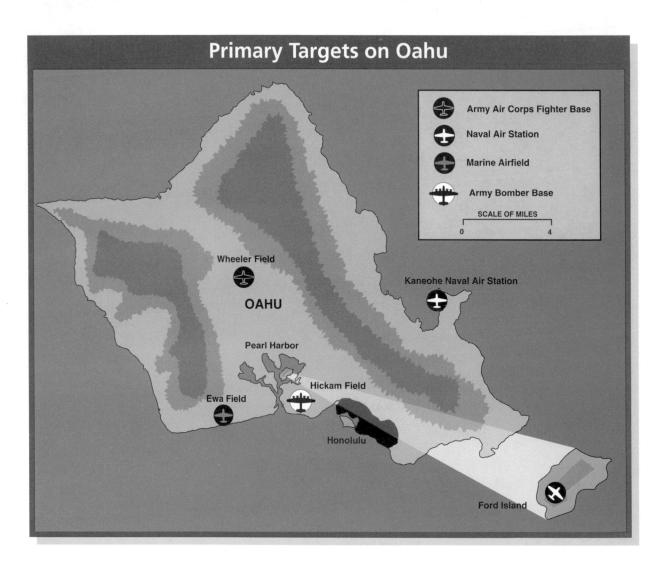

Primary Targets on Oahu

Army Air Corps Fighter Base

Naval Air Station

Marine Airfield

Army Bomber Base

SCALE OF MILES

0   4

Wheeler Field

OAHU

Kaneohe Naval Air Station

Pearl Harbor

Hickam Field

Ewa Field

Honolulu

Ford Island

dive-bombers would close out the mission by attacking any carriers left afloat and any chance targets.

Under Way to Infamy

Shimizu's Sixth Fleet submarines started departing Japanese bases in mid-November. Nagumo's carriers and escorting vessels gathered at Etorofu as planned and commenced their eastward voyage to infamy on November 26.

Meanwhile, Japanese and American diplomats continued to hold peace discussions in Washington, D.C.

CHAPTER THREE

Countdown

It now seems reasonable to conclude that the most surprising aspect of Japan's surprise attack on Pearl Harbor is that it came as a surprise. Evidence of Japanese intent abounded. But multiple warnings of Japan's impending actions went unnoticed or unheeded. Why? The answer now lies only slightly obscured by the trappings of old intrigues, misconceptions, and miscommunications.

First Warning

By early November 1941, officials at the American embassy in Tokyo were alarmed by what they judged to be an atmosphere of growing Japanese hostility toward the United States. General Hideki Tojo, a well-known militarist and leader of Japan's Kodo-Ha war party, had been named prime minister and ordered to form a new cabinet on October 18, 1941. After evaluating Japan's new government for two weeks, Joseph C. Grew, the American ambassador in Japan, concluded that Tojo's regime might seek a military solution.

On November 3, more than three weeks before *Kido Butai* left Etoforu, Grew sent a cautionary note to the U.S. Department of State. He warned that Japan might mount

> an all-out, do-or-die attempt to render Japan impervious to foreign embargoes, even risking hari kiri [suicide] rather than cede to foreign pressure. . . . Japan's resort to measures which might make war with the United States inevitable might come with dramatic and dangerous suddenness.

General Hideki Tojo was named prime minister of Japan on October 18, 1941. U.S. officials worried that Tojo, a notorious militarist, would resort to war to resolve hostilities between Japan and the United States.

O n April 16, 1941, Secretary of State Cordell Hull presented his real "basis for negotiations" to Admiral Kichisaburo Nomura, the Japanese ambassador in Washington. Hull's plan for developing a peaceful resolution to the mounting differences between Japan and the United States focused on four elements. Throughout the long months of negotiations between the two nations, the United States held fast to the spirit of Hull's Four Principles:

1. Respect for the territorial integrity and sovereignty of each and all nations;

2. Support of the principle of noninterference in the internal affairs of other countries;

3. Support of the principle of equality, including equality of commercial opportunity;

4. Nondisturbance of the status quo in the Pacific except as the status quo may be altered by peaceful means.

Hull always doubted Japan's peaceful intentions. But he believed that if the Japanese government "should make up its mind to abandon its . . . policies of force and invasion and adopt a peaceful course with worthwhile international relationships, it could find no objection to these four points reasonably applied."

The Limits of Friendship

The Japanese, of course, had already decided earlier (at the Imperial Conference in Tokyo on September 6) to go to war with the United States "when necessary." The Combined Fleet had accepted that decision as permission to implement its plan to attack Pearl Harbor. Yet differences of opinion as to exactly what was meant by "when necessary" persisted among Japan's leaders until late October. Tojo, as prime minister, quickly felt the weight of his new office and wanted to proceed slowly. He insisted that more time should be taken to study the situation. But General Gen Sugiyama and Admiral Osami Nagano, chiefs of the army and navy general staffs, respectively, wanted an immediate decision. A conference held in Tokyo on October 30 finally approved a program for continuing a diplomatic dialogue with the United States. This program later became known as Proposal A.

Proposal A, in brief, asserted that Japan would continue to observe all conditions of the Tripartite Pact; would not withdraw troops from either China or French Indochina (but would negotiate over China while keeping troops there for twenty-five years); and would not accept the Four Principles set forth on April 16, 1941, by U.S. secretary of state Cordell Hull (which called for Japan to respect the rights and sovereignty of all nations; to not interfere in the internal affairs of other countries; to support the principle of equality, especially in trade; and to maintain the status quo in the Pacific). Japan did agree to the principle of equality in trading with China provided that the principle applied equally to the rest of the world.

On November 4, Foreign Minister Shigenori Togo dispatched a copy of Proposal A to Ambassador Admiral Kichisaburo Nomura in Washington, D.C. Togo added a note that said, in part:

> This time we are showing the limit of our friendship; this time we are making our last possible bargain, and I hope we can thus settle all our trouble with the United States peaceably.
>
> . . . lest anything go awry, I want you to follow my instructions to the letter . . . there will be no room for personal interpretation.

Before Nomura had time to digest the contents of Proposal A, Togo followed with Proposal B. The foreign minister instructed Nomura to present the second proposal if there seemed "to be a remarkable difference between the Japanese and American views."

Nomura, a sincere man, enjoyed a pleasant relationship with Hull and had earned the secretary's respect. But Nomura's role in a diplomatic cat-and-mouse game forced him to become less than forthright in his dealings with the American. To act in devious ways contrary to his nature began to wear on Nomura, so much so that he offered to resign as ambassador. Only his loyalty to the emperor persuaded Nomura to continue to represent Japan in the critical negotiations with the United States.

The next day, November 5, Togo levied an even greater burden on Nomura by setting a deadline for the heretofore open-ended peace talks:

> Because of various circumstances, it is absolutely necessary that all arrangements for the signing of this agreement be completed by the 25th of this month. I realize that this is a difficult order, but under the circumstances it is an unavoidable one.

The twenty-fifth was selected because the *Kido Butai* was scheduled to leave Etoforu on November 26 (November 25, Washington time). If the United States accepted the latest Japanese offer before the fleet sailed, Japan would realize substantial savings in time, fuel, and personnel.

Alarming Predictions

When Nomura presented Proposal A to the U.S. secretary of state on November 7, Hull already knew the contents of Japan's latest diplomatic offering. Through the tireless efforts of American code breakers, the Japanese diplomatic code—the so-called Purple

Relations between U.S. Secretary of State Cordell Hull (left) and Ambassador Kichisaburo Nomura (right) deteriorated during the 1941 peace negotiations.

Code—had been broken in August 1940. Since then, American cryptanalysts (experts in deciphering coded messages) had been routinely intercepting and decoding Japanese diplomatic messages. Hull, though cordial as always to Nomura, dismissed the document as containing nothing "fundamentally new or offering any real recessions from the position consistently maintained by the Japanese Government."

Later that afternoon, Hull attended a meeting of Roosevelt's cabinet. Apparently fearing the breakdown of diplomatic efforts to prevent war, Hull warned the president and other cabinet members of "the dangers of the international situation." Hull went on to brief them on Japan's latest proposal, stressing that in his view "relations were extremely critical and that we should be on the lookout for a military attack anywhere by Japan at any time." Inasmuch as the Japanese naval general staff and the Combined Fleet had just initiated their operational orders, Hull's warning displayed his remarkable grasp of the situation.

On that same day, as if to add an exclamation point to Hull's warning, Admiral Harold R. Stark, chief of naval operations, ended a letter to Admiral Husband E. Kimmel in Pearl Harbor with an even more remarkable prediction: "Things seem to be moving steadily toward a crisis in the Pacific. . . . A month may see, literally, most anything." One month later fell precisely on the calendar date of December 7, 1941.

In a letter to Admiral Kimmel on November 7, 1941, Admiral Harold R. Stark (pictured), chief of naval operations, predicted that negotiations with Japan would reach their climax within a month.

"Please Fight Harder"

In a November 15 message to Ambassador Nomura, Foreign Minister Togo reaffirmed November 25 as the cutoff date for negotiations:

> You may be sure that you have all my gratitude for the efforts you have put forth, but the fate of our Empire hangs by the slender thread of a few days, so please fight harder than you ever did before. . . . In your opinion we ought to wait and see what turn the war takes and remain patient. . . . However . . . the situation renders this out of the question. I set the deadline for the solution of these negotiations in my #736 [message], and there will be no change.

Togo's foreign ministry also sent instructions to the Japanese embassy in Washington (and to other diplomatic missions) for destroying code machines in the event of an emergency.

The Magicians

The Japanese could never believe that the Americans were smart enough to break their complex diplomatic cipher known as the Purple Code. But a team of U.S. Signal Intelligence Service (SIS) cryptanalysts (code breakers) proved that it never pays to underestimate an enemy. Under the astute and untiring leadership of Lieutenant Colonel William F. Friedman, the Americans broke the Purple Code in August 1940, after more than eighteen months of exhaustive labor.

Japan's diplomatic service used several codes—the Purple Code, and multiple versions of the so-called J Code—to send messages from the foreign ministry in Tokyo to embassies and consulates overseas, including the consulate in Honolulu. From the summer of 1940 on, U.S. analysts were routinely intercepting and decoding Japanese diplomatic messages. By the fall of 1941, U.S. officials knew more about Japanese intentions than Ambassador Kichisaburo Nomura did, in that Tokyo gave Nomura his information on a need-to-know basis.

However, access to Japanese diplomatic codes did not reveal all of Tokyo's aims to U.S. officials. The Japanese army and navy initiated much of their government's strategies and policies, and the Americans had not yet broken Japan's naval codes. Thus Washington did not

Lieutenant Colonel William F. Friedman was called upon to decipher Japan's Purple Code. Here, Friedman explains the principles of an intricate ciphering machine to an assistant.

know of Yamamoto's plan to attack Pearl Harbor. But U.S. code breakers would crack that cipher too in a few months.

Because the project dedicated to breaking the Japanese Purple and J Codes was aptly named "Magic," it follows that the analysts who performed the wizardry might reasonably be called "Magicians."

That same day, Special Envoy Saburo Kurusu arrived in Washington from Tokyo, supposedly to assist Nomura in his ongoing negotiations. Japan's purpose in sending a special envoy to Washington at that time, other than to distract American officials from Japan's real intentions, remains a source of wonder. Nor is it clear how much, if anything, Kurusu knew about Japanese plans for the next few weeks. Perhaps Foreign Minister Togo sent Kurusu to Washington merely to assure that Nomura would "fight harder."

Japan's primary negotiators, Special Envoy Kurusu (left) and Ambassador Nomura (right), hoped they could peacefully solve the problems facing Japan and the United States.

Second Warning

On November 17, as Yamamoto and *Kido Butai* personnel in Hitokappu Bay (Etorofu) hoisted toasts to a Japanese success at Pearl Harbor, Ambassador Grew in Tokyo sent a second clear warning to U.S. secretary of state Cordell Hull:

> In emphasizing the need for guarding against sudden military or naval actions by Japan in areas not at present involved in the China conflict, I am taking into account as a possibility that the Japanese would exploit all available tactical advantages, including that of initiative and surprise. It is important, however, that our Government not (repeat not) place upon us . . . major responsibility for giving prior warning . . . [as] our field of military and naval observation is almost literally restricted to what can be seen with our own eyes, which is negligible.

A Helpful Hint

On that same day in Washington, D.C., Nomura introduced Kurusu to President Franklin Roosevelt and Secretary of State Cordell Hull. Kurusu, a veteran Japanese diplomat, had served earlier as Japan's chief negotiator of the Tripartite Pact. Hull's first impression of the small envoy wearing glasses and a neat mustache was one of immediate distrust. Hull wrote in his memoirs:

> Neither his appearance nor his attitude commanded confidence or respect. I felt from the start that he was deceitful. . . . His only recommendation in my eyes was that he spoke excellent English, having married his American secretary.

That evening Nomura and Kurusu paid an informal visit to Postmaster General Frank C. Walker. Although Walker served in no official diplomatic capacity, he took a keen interest in the peace negotiations. He and Nomura liked each other and shared a mutual respect. Each used the other as an unofficial sounding board for receiving and interpreting vibrations given off by the diplomatic maneuverings of their respective governments. On this occasion, Walker hinted to Nomura that a show of goodwill by Japan might aid the cause of peace. Walker said (as quoted by Nomura):

> The President is very desirous of an understanding between Japan and the United States. . . . If Japan would now do something real, such as evacuating French Indo-China [Vietnam], showing her peaceful intentions, the way would open up for us to furnish you with oil and it would probably lead to the re-establishment of normal trade relations. The Secretary of State cannot bring public opinion in line so long as you do not take some real and definite steps to reassure the Americans.

Nomura acted quickly on Walker's hint, and he and Kurusu met with Hull the next morning (November 18). During a three-hour meeting, Nomura suggested to Hull that Japan might be willing to withdraw its troops from French Indochina if the United States agreed to lift its embargo and unfreeze Japanese assets.

Hull received Nomura's offer without enthusiasm, pointing out that troops withdrawn from Indochina might be "diverted to some equally objectionable movement elsewhere." Nevertheless, the secretary, recognizing the potential for a continuing dialogue, and thus a reasonable solution to their problems, promised to consider the Japanese proposal. But Nomura felt that Hull had rejected the offer and notified Foreign Minister Togo of its rejection. Togo cabled Nomura to present Proposal B.

The Winds of War

On November 19, while Nomura and Kurusu prepared to present Proposal B in a meeting with Hull the next day, Tokyo dispatched to its Washington embassy (and its other embassies) the now-famous "Winds" messages. The messages established a system for warning Japanese diplomatic posts of an imminent break in relations by including coded "weather reports" in the daily Japanese language shortwave news broadcasts and general intelligence broadcasts.

In short, to warn that Japanese relations were about to be severed with the United States, the weather forecast would be "east wind, rain"; with the USSR, "north wind, cloudy"; and with Great Britain, "west wind, clear."

The "Winds" messages were intercepted and deciphered by U.S. code breakers. A continuous twenty-four-hour radio watch on the military listening networks was initiated in anticipation of intercepting an "east wind" message. Historians still dispute whether that message was ever broadcast by the Japanese or intercepted by the Americans. In either case, such a message would not have disclosed anything new to the Americans. Whether the "east wind, rain" message was ever broadcast or heard remains one of history's great intrigues.

Proposal B

On November 20, Ambassador Nomura presented Proposal B to Secretary of State Hull. Stanley K. Hornbeck, adviser to the State Department for Far Eastern affairs, summarized the lengthy proposal as Japanese requests:

> that the United States agree to cease giving aid to China; that the U.S. desist from [increasing] its military force in the Pacific; that the United States help Japan obtain products of the Netherlands East Indies; that the United States undertake to resume commercial relations with Japan; that the United States undertake to supply Japan "a required quantity of oil"; while Japan on her part would be free to continue her military operation in and against China and to keep her troops in Indochina and to attack the Soviet Union, would have her funds unfrozen, would be able to buy with comparative freedom from the United States, would be assured adequate supplies of oil, and would be under no obligation to remove her troops from Indochina until she should have completed her conquest of China or there had been established "in the Pacific area" conditions of peace satisfactory to her.

In Cordell Hull's assessment of the Japanese document, he stated, "The Japanese proposal of November 20 . . . was of so preposterous [absurd] a character that no responsible American official could ever have dreamed of accepting it." Yet he did not reject the proposal out of hand. He needed to buy time for the U.S. armed forces to shore up their defenses. And he needed time to prepare a counterproposal that might at last preserve peace.

The Roosevelt Modus Vivendi

Japan's latest attempt to reach a peaceful agreement with the United States apparently impressed President Roosevelt more than it had Hull. After reviewing Proposal B, Roosevelt roughed out a modus vivendi, or compromise, of his own and sent it to Hull for formalizing. Roosevelt's pencil draft covered four principles to be acted upon over the next six months:

1. U.S. to resume economic relations—some oil and rice now—more later.

2. Japan to send no more troops to Indochina or Manchurian border or any place South—(Dutch, Brit. or Siam [Thailand]).

3. Japan to agree not to invoke tripartite pact even if U.S. gets into European war.

4. U.S. to introduce Japs to Chinese to talk things over but U.S. to take no part in their conversations. . . .

Later on Pacific agreements.

Roosevelt's compromise offer represented a real hope for a peaceful solution to the problems between the two nations.

Kurusu, recognizing the importance still placed upon the Tripartite Pact by the Americans, delivered a letter to the Department of State the next day. The letter declared that his government

would never project the people of Japan into war at the behest of any foreign power: it will accept warfare only as the ultimate, inescapable necessity for the maintenance of its security and the preservation of national life against inactive justice.

But Hull trusted neither Kurusu nor the government he represented. The next day, November 22, U.S. code breakers intercepted a message from Tokyo to Nomura, confirming Hull's suspicions. The message extended the deadline for negotiations to November 29 and warned: "THIS TIME WE MEAN IT, THAT THE DEADLINE ABSOLUTELY CANNOT BE CHANGED. AFTER THAT THINGS ARE AUTOMATICALLY GOING TO HAPPEN."

That evening, Nomura and Kurusu called on Hull to urge a hasty reply to Proposal B. Hull replied with obvious irritation. "There is no reason why any demand should be made on us. I am quite disappointed that despite all my efforts you are still trying to railroad through your demand for our reply." He did, however, promise a reply as soon as possible, intending to answer with a formalized version of Roosevelt's modus vivendi.

"A Dream Come True"

On that same day (November 23 in Japan), the personnel of *Kido Butai* learned of their destination. They would leave in three days. Seaman Iki Kuramoto expressed the attitude that prevailed among his shipmates when he wrote:

An air attack on HAWAII! A dream come true. . . . What will the people at home think when they hear the news? Won't

After reviewing Japan's Proposal B, President Franklin Roosevelt drafted his modus vivendi, a compromise offer to ease Japanese-American conflicts.

they be excited! I can see them clapping their hands and shouting for joy. These were our feelings. We would teach the arrogant Anglo-Saxon scoundrels a lesson.

Meanwhile, peace negotiations continued in Washington.

Hull's Ten Points

On November 24, Hull met with representatives of Great Britain, China, Australia, and the Netherlands to review copies of Roosevelt's modus vivendi. China, with British support, expressed concerns that in the compromise America was "inclined to appease Japan at the expense of China."

Secretary of War Henry L. Stimson called President Roosevelt on the morning of November 26 to inform him that a Japanese fleet had been sighted sailing southward off Formosa (Taiwan). The fleet of some thirty to fifty vessels reportedly carried five divisions of combat troops. Upon hearing the news, Roosevelt "fairly blew up."

The president said:

> That changed the whole situation because it was evidence of bad faith on the part of the Japanese that while they were negotiating for an entire truce—an entire withdrawal—they would be sending this expedition down there to Indo-China.

Roosevelt then abandoned his proposed plan.

The secretary of state was left without a reply to Japan's Proposal B. Consequently, Hull and his staff hastily put together an answer for Nomura and Kurusu. The diplomatic note became known as the "Hull Note" or Ten Points. This long document basically restated the American position that had not varied in months. Although the note was firm, Hull said later that "there was nothing in there that any peaceful nation pursuing a peaceful course would not have been delighted to accept." Nomura and Kurusu did not agree.

Tokyo interpreted Hull's note as an ultimatum. In turn, Washington perceived Tokyo's reaction to the note as a further indication of Japan's continuing refusal to negotiate in good faith. The threat of war loomed greater than ever on November 26.

Washington Warns Pearl Harbor

On November 27, with the diplomatic picture drawing grim in Washington, Army Chief of Staff George C. Marshall alerted his top commander in Pearl Harbor to the worsening situation. Marshall's War Department Message No. 472 to Lieutenant General Walter C. Short said:

> Negotiations with Japan appear to be terminated to all practical purposes with only the barest possibilities that the

Japanese Government might come back and offer to continue. Japanese action unpredictable but hostile action possible at any moment. If hostilities cannot, repeat cannot, be avoided the United States desires that Japan commit the first overt act. This policy should not, repeat not, be construed as restricting you to a course of action that might jeopardize your defense. Prior to hostile Japanese action you are directed to undertake such reconnaissance and other measures as you deem necessary but these measures should be carried out so as not, repeat not, to alarm civil population or disclose intent. Report measures taken. Should hostilities occur you will carry out the tasks assigned in Rainbow Five [the army's basic war plan] so far as they apply to Japan. Limit [circulation] of this highly secret information to minimum essential officers.

On November 27, 1941, Army Chief of Staff George C. Marshall alerted officials in Pearl Harbor to increasing hostilities with Japan and gave them instructions in the event of war.

Admiral Harold R. Stark, chief of naval operations, dispatched an even stronger message to Admiral Husband E. Kimmel, part of which follows:

This despatch is to be considered a war warning. Negotiations with Japan looking toward stabilization of conditions in the Pacific have ceased and an aggressive move by Japan is expected within a few days. The number and equipment of Japanese troops and the organization of the naval task forces [indicate] an amphibious expedition against either the Philippines Thai or Kra Peninsula or possibly Borneo. Execute an appropriate defense deployment preparatory to carrying out the tasks assigned in WPL 46 [the navy's basic war plan]. Inform district and army authorities. A similar warning is being sent by the War Department.

Following the receipt of these war warnings, a rash of misconceptions and miscommunications broke out among top army and navy commanders at Pearl Harbor. Much of the confusion resulted from a divided command in Hawaii and the failure of leaders of both services to understand their basic responsibilities. The army's basic mission was to defend Pearl Harbor and the Hawaiian Islands, whereas the navy's primary task was to deter Japanese aggression in the western Pacific. Their responsibilities often tended to overlap.

For example, the army was tasked to defend Pearl Harbor, but responsibility for long-range aerial reconnaissance fell to the navy. Conversely, the navy was not tasked to defend Pearl Harbor, yet the army mistakenly considered ships in port to form a part of the Hawaiian defenses. Misunderstandings, communication gaps, and the blurred lines of overlapping responsibilities resulted in a wanton lack of preparedness at Pearl Harbor—despite the clear warnings.

The Monkey Wrench

On November 28, 1941, President Franklin D. Roosevelt met in Washington with his top civilian and military advisers. The president called the meeting to discuss the strategic implications of a recently sighted Japanese fleet heading toward Indochina. The key figures in attendance were the cabinet secretaries Hull, Knox, and Stimson, and the joint chiefs of staff Marshall and Stark. Secretary of War Stimson later recorded notes on that meeting in his diary.

It was the consensus that . . . an Expeditionary Force on the sea of about 25,000 Japanese troops aimed for a landing somewhere . . . changed the situation . . . [as to] whether or not we should address an ultimatum to Japan about moving the troops which she already had on land in Indo-China. It was now the opinion of everyone that if this expedition was allowed to get around the southern point of Indo-China and to get off and land in the Gulf of Siam, either at Bangkok or further west, it would be a terrific blow at all of the three Powers, Britain at Singapore, the Netherlands, and ourselves in the Philippines. It was the consensus of everybody that this must not be allowed.

Japan's latest move toward Indochina did little to encourage the success of diplomatic negotiations in Washington. In a telephone conversation with a Japanese foreign minister in Tokyo, Special Envoy Saburo Kurusu said, "As before [when Japan's move on Indochina in July 1941 triggered an economic freeze by the United States], that southern matter . . . was the monkey wrench."

"Climb Mount Niitaka"

On December 1, at five minutes after two o'clock in the afternoon, Premier Hideki Tojo stood before Emperor Hirohito and a gathering of Japan's supreme civil and military leaders in Room One East of the Imperial Palace in Tokyo. With a grim face and grave voice, Tojo told his listeners that Japan should not give in to American demands to vacate China and abort the Tripartite Pact. To do so, he warned, would be to threaten Japan's very existence. "Matters have reached the point where Japan must begin war with the United States, Great Britain and the Netherlands to preserve her empire." The prime minister proceeded to recount the long history of unsuccessful Japanese-American negotiations.

The ensuing spirited debate covered a range of problems—public morale, economic and financial considerations, national security, oil and raw materials, and other emergency precautions such as food supplies; finally, war documents were signed by all present. Emperor Hirohito, in his private chambers, became the last to affix his signature, thus signifying his formal approval of Japan's decision to go to war.

At 1730 the next day, December 2, Admiral Isoroku Ya-mamoto dispatched a message to *Kido Butai*: *"Niitaka yama nobure ichi-ne-rei-ya"* ("Climb Mount Niitaka, 1208"). This meant to proceed with the attack on Pearl Harbor on December 8 (December 7 in Hawaii).

Mount Niitaka, on Formosa, was the highest mountain in the Japanese empire, higher even than Mount Fuji. Yamamoto's message symbolized the mountainous task that lay before Japan. It would be a long, steep climb . . . and a swift, dizzying descent.

Point of Attack

At 1130 on December 6, *Kido Butai* corrected course to 180 degrees due south toward Hawaii and advanced speed to twenty knots. Ten minutes later, Admiral Chuichi Nagumo ordered the historic Z flag hoisted on *Akagi*. It was the same flag that Admiral Togo had raised thirty-six years earlier during the Russo-Japanese War to signify the Japanese victory over the Russian czar's forces at Tsushima. *Akagi* then signaled a message from Yamamoto to encourage another great Japanese victory: "The rise and fall of the Empire depends upon this battle. Every man will do his duty."

On December 1, 1941, Emperor Hirohito (pictured) signed documents declaring war on the United States. (Above) As war draws near, crewmen aboard a Japanese aircraft carrier prepare to launch their attack.

"A Sacred Duty"

On Saturday, December 6, 1941—X day minus one—while *Kido Butai* steamed steadily eastward, President Franklin D. Roosevelt approved the draft of a letter to Emperor Hirohito. He sent it to Secretary of State Cordell Hull for finalizing and forwarding to Ambassador Joseph C. Grew in Tokyo. The president's letter, which was to have been delivered to Emperor Hirohito on December 7 (December 8 in Tokyo), is partially shown below:

> During the past few weeks it has become clear to the world that Japanese military, naval, and air forces have been sent to southern Indo-China in such large numbers as to create a reasonable doubt . . . that this continuing concentration in Indo-China is not defensive in its character. . . .

I address myself to Your Majesty at this moment in the fervent hope that Your Majesty may, as I am doing, give thought in this definite emergency to ways of dispelling the dark clouds [of an impending military attack]. I am confident that both of us, for the sake of the peoples of not only our own great countries but for the sake of the humanity in neighboring territories, have a sacred duty to restore traditional amity and prevent further death and destruction in the world.

Because of a Japanese-initiated administrative delay on all diplomatic cables, Hirohito did not receive Roosevelt's message until after the war had started. There is nothing to indicate that an earlier delivery would have significantly altered history.

The warriors of *Kido Butai* filled the air with cheers. Far to the west, thousands of other Japanese warriors moved into position and stood by in readiness to invade areas ranging from the Philippines to Singapore to the Dutch East Indies. Meanwhile, only hours before Admiral Yamamoto's X day, Japanese and American diplomats continued peace negotiations in Washington, D.C.

That night, Nagumo received some disappointing news. Ensign Takeo Yoshikawa, a spy who had been posing as a vice consul at the Japanese consulate in Honolulu since April 1941, reported that no carriers were harbored in Pearl Harbor as of 1800 on December 6. (Admiral Kimmel had deployed the carriers *Enterprise* and *Lexington* to sea after receiving Stark's warning message.) Among those most disappointed by the news were Commander Minoru Genda, the air operations officer, and Commander Mitsuo Fuchida, the designated leader of the air attack on Pearl Harbor.

Fuchida arose aboard *Akagi* at 0500 on Sunday, December 7, 1941—X day. He dressed, carefully donning red underwear and a red shirt beneath his flying clothes, and then joined Lieutenant

Shigeharu Murata in the officers' mess, or dining area. Murata, leader of the torpedo-bomber attack wave, wore similar red underclothing. Both men selected the undergarments to hide any show of blood that might dishearten their followers. Murata smiled at Fuchida.

"Good morning, Commander," he said. "Honolulu sleeps."

Fuchida sat next to him and asked, "How do you know?"

"The Honolulu radio plays soft music. Everything is fine," Murata answered. And the two pilots ate what they both considered might well be their last breakfast.

Kido Butai had crossed more than three thousand miles of frigid, storm-tossed waters in the North Pacific without discovery. Just before daybreak, Nagumo's fleet reached the outer periphery of its designated launch point—26 degrees north latitude, 158 degrees west longitude—some 275 miles due north of Pearl Harbor.

On *Akagi's* bridge, Admiral Nagumo turned to Commander Genda and quietly said, "I have brought the task force successfully to the point of attack. From now on the burden is on your shoulders and the rest of the flying group."

"Admiral, I am sure the airmen will succeed," Genda replied.

★ ★ ★ ★ ★ ★ ★ ★ ★ ★ ★ ★ ★

CHAPTER FOUR

"This Is No Drill"

On December 7, 1941, under murky, predawn skies, explosive-charged catapults boomed simultaneously aboard the sister cruisers *Chikuma* and *Tone* at precisely 0530. Two single-engine, Type O reconnaissance seaplanes bolted skyward and winged off over the southern horizon. *Chikuma*'s plane proceeded toward Pearl Harbor, *Tone*'s toward Lahaina Roads. Their mission was to provide advance information to the first wave of Japanese attackers.

Commander Mitsuo Fuchida and his first-wave attack aircraft would not await the return of the reconnaissance planes. Their orders were to follow a half hour behind the seaplanes and receive the reconnaissance reports by radio while en route to the target.

By 0550, Nagumo's six carriers had drawn within 220 miles of Oahu. The admiral ordered them turned to the wind for launching aircraft. Captain Kiichi Hasegawa, *Akagi*'s skipper, spoke briefly to his assembled pilots. "All right, the plans are made," he concluded, "let's get going!"

Heavy swells showered flight decks with salt spray, as the carriers turned eastward, pitching and heaving into a stiff wind. Flight decks tilted from 11 to 15 degrees. A 5-degree list was sufficient to cancel takeoffs under normal circumstances, but not today. The rough seas delayed takeoff twenty minutes.

A concerned Commander Shogo Masuda, *Akagi*'s air officer, greeted Fuchida at the carrier's command post on the upper flight deck. "What about this rough sea?" he asked. Both officers knew that there was no time to revise the carefully laid plans.

(Above) Japanese pilots rush to their planes as Kido Butai approaches Oahu while (left) others start their ascent in Kate torpedo bombers. (Below) Meanwhile, bomber pilots receive last-minute instructions before taking off for Pearl Harbor.

"I have already given the word for action," Fuchida replied and after saying his good-byes to those present, left to board his aircraft for the most important flight of his life.

Appointment with Infamy

Prior to boarding his aircraft, each pilot readied himself for battle by tying around his head a *hachimaki* (headband) bearing the word *Hisso* (certain victory). The carrier's senior maintenance officer presented a specially made white *hachimaki* to Fuchida. As he handed it to Fuchida, the officer said, "All of the maintenance crew mem-

As *Kido Butai* steamed closer to Oahu and launch time drew near, Commander Kyozo Ohashi, senior staff officer of the Fifth Carrier Division, sat in *Shokaku's* operations room wondering what the next few hours would bring. He worried about how his young, inexperienced pilots would perform in combat. Ohashi separated the feelings of his officers and flight crews into three classes:

First, there were those who were virtually unmoved by the special mission of attacking Pearl Harbor, who considered the operation as their God-given duty, and who faced the immediate future with grim [indifference]. Into this class fell most of the older staff officers and key pilots.

Secondly, there were those who thought the Pearl Harbor operation would succeed, but were apprehensive about the final outcome of the war. They wondered what was going to happen after the initial phase was over. Into this class fell the more intelligent of the younger officers who tried to look at things from a long-range viewpoint.

Finally, there were those who were nervous and afraid of what lay ahead. This class included the newer officers, the young trainees, and those of the crew who could only glimpse snatches of the overall plan.

bers would like to go along to Pearl Harbor. But since we cannot, please take this *hachimaki* from us as a symbol that we are with you in spirit." Fuchida bowed and thanked him warmly, touched and humbled by the gesture from those whom he and his pilots depended on for so much. He wrapped the scarf securely over his helmet.

All six carriers launched in unison shortly after 0600. The fighters lifted off first. With a one-man crew and no bomb load, they required only a short run to become airborne. Lieutenant Commander Shigeharu Itaya led the sleek fighters off *Akagi's* deck, dropping suddenly out of sight. Lieutenant Seizo Ofuchi, acting as takeoff officer, held his breath. What an evil omen it would be if the first plane to take off should plunge into the sea. "But he made it and soared upward like a great bird," Ofuchi recalled.

One hundred and eighty-four aircraft followed. One fighter crashed on takeoff. Engine trouble forced a second fighter to stay behind. Fifty-one Aichi D3A "Val" dive-bombers; 40 Nakajima B5N "Kate" torpedo bombers; 49 horizontal bombers, also Kates (which served a dual role); and 43 Mitsubishi A6M "Zero" fighters made up Fuchida's first attack wave. Within a record time of fifteen minutes, 183 aircraft took to the air, formed up, and climbed above a cloud layer to an altitude of ten thousand feet. At about 0620, on Fuchida's signal, Japan's winged samurai turned toward Oahu and an appointment with infamy.

The Crowded Sky

Fuchida's air fleet was not the only group of aircraft heading toward Pearl Harbor that morning. At 0615, Vice Admiral William F. "Bull" Halsey had launched eighteen Douglas SBD Dauntless dive-bombers off the U.S. carrier *Enterprise*. The carrier, along with three heavy cruisers and nine destroyers, made up Halsey's Task Force Eight. Halsey had just delivered some marine aircraft to Wake Island and was homeward bound. He was due back in the Pearl Harbor channel at 0730, but rough waters had delayed refueling his destroyers. When dawn found him still two hundred miles from port, he drew a mix of SBDs from Scouting and Bombing Squadron Six and sent them on ahead to scout the waters.

Two of the eighteen SBDs, led by Commander Howard L. Young, the *Enterprise* air group commander, sped off at once toward Pearl Harbor. Lieutenant Commander Bromfield Nichol, one of Halsey's aides, rode along as a passenger with Young. Because Task Force Eight was maintaining strict radio silence at sea, Nichol was to hand-carry Halsey's operations report to fleet commander in chief Kimmel. The remaining sixteen SBDs, led by Lieutenant Commander Halstead Hopping, formed up and followed Young's SBDs at 0637.

At 0615, Vice Admiral William F. Halsey (pictured) launched eighteen Douglas SBD Dauntless dive-bombers (above) from the carrier Enterprise, *which was en route to Pearl Harbor.*

Meanwhile, approximately one hundred miles east of Oahu, the day dawned behind a flight of twelve new Boeing B-17E bombers. Fresh from the factory, the American heavy bombers belonged to the Thirty-eighth and Eighty-eighth Reconnaissance Squadrons. Flying out of Hamilton Field, California, they were being ferried to Clarke Field in the Philippines under the command of Major Truman H. Landon. Landon's flight plan called for a refueling stopover at Hickam Field, adjacent to Pearl Harbor, with an estimated time of arrival set at 0800. Nearing the end of a long, fourteen-hour flight from the mainland, Landon's immediate concern was reaching Hickam before running out of gas.

Some two hundred miles to the north of Pearl Harbor, Admiral Nagumo ordered sixteen more reconnaissance planes aloft at 0630, four each from his battleships and heavy cruisers. Discovery by American ships or planes at this critical point might prove fatal to his fleet—and to the future of the Japanese empire.

The sky over Oahu was about to become crowded.

First Shot

While aircraft of both nations were still converging on Oahu, the twenty-five submarines of Vice Admiral Mitsumi Shimizu's Sixth Fleet had already fanned out into preassigned positions at the entrance to Pearl Harbor. The U.S. destroyer *Ward* was patrolling a two-mile square near the mouth of the harbor. At 0357, Lieutenant William W. Outerbridge, who had been *Ward*'s commander for

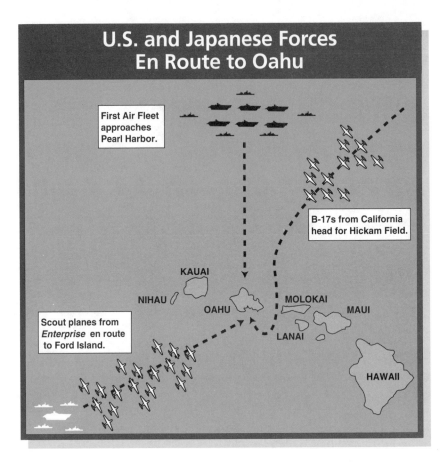

U.S. and Japanese Forces En Route to Oahu

First Air Fleet approaches Pearl Harbor.

B-17s from California head for Hickam Field.

Scout planes from *Enterprise* en route to Ford Island.

KAUAI

NIHAU

OAHU

MOLOKAI

MAUI

LANAI

HAWAII

only two days, received a blinker message from the mine-sweeper *Condor:*

SIGHTED SUBMERGED SUBMARINE ON WESTERLY COURSE, SPEED 9 KNOTS.

Outerbridge ordered general quarters (an alert for battle stations to be manned) and took up pursuit of the submarine. After an unsuccessful search, the fledgling skipper secured from general quarters (called for the crew to retire from battle stations) at 0435. Lieutenant (j.g.) Oscar W. Goepner took over as officer of the deck.

At 0630, *Antares*, a stores and supply ship, spotted the same submarine trying to slip into the harbor through the antitorpedo netting, which had been opened earlier to admit two mine-sweepers. *Antares* blinked a warning signal to *Ward*. Goepner roused the captain, who again sounded general quarters. By then it was 0640.

Ward knifed full ahead through the water toward the sub and commenced firing within fifty yards of the intruder. Lieutenant Outerbridge recalled that the first shot "missed, passing directly over the conning tower." The next round hit the submarine "at the waterline . . . [close to] the junction of the hull and conning tower." The vessel, keeling "over to starboard . . . appeared to slow and sink." *Ward* dumped "a full pattern of depth charges" set to explode at one hundred feet. "The submarine sank in about 1200 feet of water."

Ward reported the submarine sunk at 0700. Fifty-five minutes were still to elapse before 183 Japanese aircraft arrived over Oahu to strike with devastating fury from the air. Thus, oddly enough, American sailors rather than Japanese airmen fired the first shot at Pearl Harbor. And the Japanese shed first blood.

Crew members of the destroyer Ward *pose near one of the ship's guns. The destroyer, which fired the first shot on December 7th, successfully sank a Japanese submarine as it approached the entrance of Pearl Harbor.*

Nagumo Launches Second Wave

Shortly before 0700, Lieutenant Fusata Iida, leader of the Third Air Control Group (of Zeros), briefed his young pilots for the last time aboard *Soryu*. "What are you going to do in case you have engine trouble in flight?" he demanded, neither expecting nor

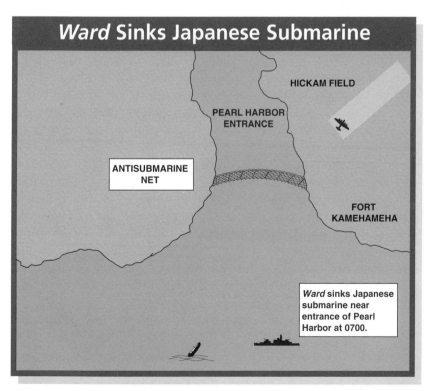

Ward Sinks Japanese Submarine

HICKAM FIELD

PEARL HARBOR
ENTRANCE

ANTISUBMARINE
NET

FORT
KAMEHAMEHA

Ward sinks Japanese submarine near entrance of Pearl Harbor at 0700.

Japanese Val dive-bombers prepare for takeoff. Seventy-eight Vals were launched during the second attack wave.

wanting an answer. Without pausing, he provided his own answer. "In case of trouble I will fly directly to my objective and make a crash dive into an enemy target rather than make an emergency landing." Such instructions left no doubt as to what was expected of them. And chance would allow several of them to so perform.

At 0705, Nagumo again ordered his carriers turned to the wind. The heavy seas had turned heavier, but nothing short of a typhoon at that point could stop Nagumo from launching his second attack wave. With visibility stretched to about twelve miles, the second attack wave began taking off at 0715 into a one-mile-high ceiling of clouds. Again, the smaller, lighter fighters flew off first, with Lieutenant Saburo Shindo leading a group of thirty-six Zeros off *Akagi*. Fifty-four Kate horizontal bombers from *Shokaku* and *Zuikaku* followed, with overall commander of the second wave, Lieutenant Commander Shigekazu Shimazaki, in the lead. Last to launch were seventy-eight Val dive-bombers, the largest single group in the entire operation, commanded by Lieutenant Commander Takashige Egusa. One dive-bomber aboard *Akagi* developed engine trouble and had to be scratched from the mission. All other aircraft took off without mishap. Launching of both the first and second waves had taken a total of ninety minutes.

Thirty-nine fighters remained behind to fly protective cover for *Kido Butai*, while 167 aircraft of the second wave sped off to the south. A combined force of 350 Japanese aircraft was now airborne and closing fast on the target. It was now 0730.

"Don't Worry About It"

At the Opana mobile radar station, 230 feet above sea level near Oahu's northern Kahuku Point, army privates Joseph L. Lockard and George E. Elliot picked up a huge blip on their radar screen at 0702. They figured that the blip represented "probably more than 50" planes. The two privates reported the blip to duty officer Lieutenant Kermit Tyler at Fort Shafter, thirty miles away. At 0720, Lockard informed Tyler "that we [have] an unusually large flight—in fact, the largest I [have] ever seen on the equipment—coming in from almost due north at 130 some miles."

Tyler mistakenly judged the blips to be the echoes of a flight (Landon's) of B-17s due to arrive from the United States. He thought about it for a moment and said, "Well, don't worry about it." Lockard had erred by not reporting that the radar blip indicated fifty or more planes. Had he done so, Tyler could not have mistaken the sighting for Landon's B-17s. Nor had Tyler, for security reasons, mentioned the B-17s to Lockard. When Tyler hung up, a switchboard operator asked him what he thought the blip was. "It's nothing," Tyler replied.

"This Means War"

On the night of December 6, President Franklin D. Roosevelt had received the first part of a fourteen-part Purple Coded transmission that the code breakers had intercepted earlier. It contained a message from Japan's foreign ministry to be delivered to Secretary of State Cordell Hull at 1300 eastern standard time (0730 Hawaiian standard time) the next day. The message clearly indicated Japan's intentions to forsake any further attempts to settle Japanese-American differences through diplomatic channels. It concluded:

> The Japanese Government regrets to have to notify hereby the American Government that in view of the attitude of the American Government it cannot but consider that it is impossible to reach an agreement through further negotiations.

After reading the message, Roosevelt turned to Harry Hopkins, his trusted adviser, and said, "This means war." The ominous message indeed indicated that war was imminent; but it did not indicate where Japan might strike first. Or when. Existing records show beyond doubt, however, that Roosevelt and his advisers strongly believed that Japan would move first against Southeast Asia.

General Marshall, army chief of staff, cabled a warning to General Short in Hawaii just before noon the next morning (just before 0630 Hawaiian time):

The Guns of Kamehameha

At Fort Kamehameha (named for Hawaii's great king and hero), Captain Frank W. Ebey, of the Fifty-fifth Coast Artillery, set up machine guns on the fort's tennis court. The guns began hammering away at Japanese planes at 0813. Colonel William J. McCarthy, Ebey's superior, arrived at the fort on Oahu Point just in time to witness a shocking sight:

A Japanese plane had just struck a tree and caromed off the first tree and struck into a wall at my right at the ordnance machine gun shed. . . . The pilot was dead . . . stuffed in the tree, but the plane was on the ground, and the engine went around the ordnance shop. In caroming off [it] struck several men who were in the road. One man was completely decapitated. Another man apparently had been hit by the props, because his legs and arms and head were off, lying right on the grass.

The downed airplane was a Zero belonging to Lieutenant Commander Shigeru Itaya's first-wave fighter group.

Japanese are presenting at one pm Eastern Standard Time today what amounts to an ultimatum. . . . Just what significance the hour set may have we do not know but be on the alert accordingly. Inform naval authorities of this communication.

A series of unpredictable and inopportune events delayed delivery of Marshall's cable. Short did not receive the warning until long past time for it to serve any useful purpose.

"Tora! Tora! Tora!"

The first attack wave droned steadily southward. Lieutenant Heita Matsumura, leader of *Hiryu*'s torpedo group, recalled viewing the splendor of the sun's arrival in the east.

Soon the eastern sky brightened and each cloud ball was distinctly marked by bright side and shadow, sunbeams coming down through breaks in the clouds straight onto the blue sea. It was the suitable dawn for the epoch-making day, I felt at the time.

The shafts of light seemed to form a giant replica of the Japanese naval flag. What better omen of a successful mission could be signaled by the gods of war?

Commander Fuchida also allowed himself to dwell briefly in the splendor of the scene and moment. He scanned the skies filled with the young eagles of Japan spread in perfect formation. How proud he felt to command them during his country's greatest undertaking. But the summons of great responsibilities could not for long be ignored. Commander Fuchida later recalled:

At seven I figured that we should reach Oahu in less than an hour. But, flying over thick clouds, we could not see the surface of the water and had no check on our drift. I switched on the radio direction finder to tune in the Honolulu radio station and soon picked up some music. By turning the antenna I found the exact direction from which the broadcast was coming and corrected our course. We had been 5° off.

Now I heard a Honolulu weather report: "Partly cloudy, with clouds mostly over the mountains. Visibility good. Wind north, ten knots."

A more favorable situation could not have been imagined. About 7:30 the clouds broke, and a long white line of coast appeared. We were over the northern tip of Oahu. It was time for our deployment.

At 0740, Fuchida found the skies over Oahu clear of American planes and antiaircraft fire. On a prearranged signal to his pilots, he shot off one flare to indicate that surprise had been achieved.

This meant that the more vulnerable torpedo bombers would spearhead the attack. Two flares—the signal for an alert defense—would have called for the dive-bombers to strike first, thus diverting attention from the slower torpedo bombers. But the torpedo bombers failed to react to Fuchida's single flare. He waited ten seconds and fired a second flare. The torpedo bombers, not having seen the first flare, deployed at once for attack. The dive-bombers had seen both flares, however, and rushed forward to strike the first blow. So much for well-laid plans.

In the resulting confusion, Fuchida had no choice except to follow the lead of his already committed aircraft. At 0749, he radioed to his planes: *"To, To, To,"* the signal to attack (*to* being the first syllable of *totsugekiseyo*, "charge"). Four minutes later, Fuchida called out another signal: *"Tora! Tora! Tora!"* ("Tiger! Tiger! Tiger!")—code words that notified the entire Japanese navy that his attack force had caught the Americans by complete surprise. Incredibly, his message stretched far across the Pacific and was received in both Tokyo and aboard Yamamoto's flagship *Nagato* in Hiroshima Bay.

Commander Mitsuo Fuchida led the air divisions of the First Air Fleet to victory in Operation Hawaii. With the cry "Tora! Tora! Tora!," *Fuchida announced that the fleet had achieved a surprise attack on Pearl Harbor.*

The air attack began simultaneously on Pearl Harbor, Fort Kamehameha, Schofield Barracks, and Ewa, Wheeler, and Hickam Fields at 0755. Sunday's calm turned to chaos in an instant. Diving aircraft screamed. Plunging bombs whined and exploded on targets with obscene sound and fury. Torpedoes streaked along whizzing paths across the heretofore still waters of Pearl Harbor, their lethal payloads directed against ships of steel and mortals of mere flesh, blood, and bones. Within minutes, billowing clouds of thick, black smoke from flaming metal climbed heavenward, in towering evidence of massive destruction.

So began the morning of America's greatest sorrow.

Battleship Row

Lieutenant Commander Shigeharu Murata, commanding forty Kate torpedo bombers, split his formation northwest of the marine base at Ewa. Two groups of eight Kates, under Lieutenants Tsuyoshi Nagai and Heita Matsumura, dove toward the west side of Pearl Harbor. And two groups of twelve Kates, led by Murata himself and Lieutenant Ichiro Kitajima, swung southeastward past Barbers Point, then circled Hickam Field in a wide north-northwestward arc, before taking dead aim on Ford Island and Battleship Row.

Seven battleships—*Nevada, Arizona, Tennessee, West Virginia, Maryland, Oklahoma*, and *California*—lay moored alongside the southeast side of Ford Island. They formed the appropriately named Battleship Row and represented the bulk of American naval power in the Pacific.

On the opposite side of the island, torpedo bombers led by Nagai and Matsumura delivered the first blow against the fleet, scoring hits on the light cruiser *Raleigh* and the old battleship *Utah*. (By then, the ancient *Utah* was used only as a radio-controlled target ship.) Both ships began to list immediately. A third ship, the light cruiser *Detroit*, escaped unscathed.

Aboard *Raleigh*, Ensign John R. Beardall Jr., awakened by the concussion, rushed topside in his red pajamas. He reached the quarterdeck just in time to see an airplane flash past. The plane "banked around to the left," he said later. "One of the first things I saw . . . was those big red balls . . . and it didn't take long to see what was going on."

Caught still in his blue pajamas while reading the morning paper, Captain R. Bentham Simons, *Raleigh*'s skipper, also scrambled above deck when he felt the concussion. He ran first to the signal bridge and "then climbed the ladder to the anti-aircraft control station." His gunners were just starting to fire. "Give those yellow bastards hell, boys!" he shouted and returned to the signal bridge to direct the action.

Japanese pilots wreaked havoc on Hickam Field, destroying barracks and equipment.

Nagai, himself having overflown *Detroit*, continued across Ford Island and the channel separating the island from Dock 1010 and let fly with a torpedo aimed at the minelayer *Oglala*.

A Japanese photograph records the destruction at Pearl Harbor as Japanese planes begin their onslaught on Battleship Row.

As luck would have it, Nagai's torpedo streaked beneath the shallow-hulled minelayer and struck the light cruiser *Helena*, berthed inboard of *Oglala*. The blast rocked *Helena* and burst the seams of *Oglala*.

At the same time, Murata's Kates flew in single file at an altitude of only 132 to 165 feet, dropping as low as 66 feet over the southeast loch. Flying overhead protective cover, Lieutenant Yoshio Shiga, leader of the Second Air Control Group of fighters, watched the action below.

> They moved so slowly they looked like ants crawling along the ground. The U.S. Fleet in the harbor looked so beautiful . . . just like toys on a child's floor—something that should not be attacked at all.

But the torpedomen thought otherwise, as Shiga remembered seeing "the splash in the water and a torpedo streaking for a battleship . . . just like a dragonfly laying an egg in the water."

The "egg" was laid by Murata. Trailing Murata's three-plane formation with three planes of his own, Lieutenant Jinichi Goto saw Murata's torpedo strike the battleship *West Virginia*. Murata's other two planes also scored hits. *West Virginia* took a total of six torpedoes and began to list at once.

Simultaneously, Goto veered off to the left and directed his own pilots to the nearby *Oklahoma*. Boring in low and slow, Goto concentrated on his speed, height, and correct release point. He recalled:

Smoke and Fire

When the Japanese aircraft struck along Battleship Row, Seaman Second Class Harlan C. Eisnaugle raced to his battle station aboard *Maryland*, "up in the superstructure just below the bridge." From there, he could see *Oklahoma*, already beginning to list. Eisnaugle later described the scene:

> Men were screaming and trying and trying to get aboard our ship and get out of the water. When I got to my gun, there were a few of the others there. We threw the gun over the side of the gun tube. And stood there cussing and crying at the Japs! You would be scared for a while and then you would get mad and cuss. After a while we finally got ammo up to our gun. But we had to put it into clips before it could be fired. I don't know how long a time this was. But the *Oklahoma* had rolled over on her side. And the harbor was pretty well afire by this time. The smoke and fire was all around us.

I was about twenty meters [66 feet] above the water when I released my torpedo. As my plane climbed up after the torpedo was off, I saw that I was even lower than the crow's nest of the great battleship. My observer reported a huge waterspout springing up from the ship's location. *"Atarimashita!"* ["It struck!"] he cried. The other two planes in my group . . . also attacked *Oklahoma*.

Their torpedoes scored the second and third of five hits on the hapless battlewagon.

"This Is No Drill"

A heartbeat after the first bomb fell on Ford Island, the Pearl Harbor signal tower notified Admiral Kimmel's headquarters of the attack by phone. The message was relayed to the admiral's home in Makalapa Heights, overlooking the naval base.

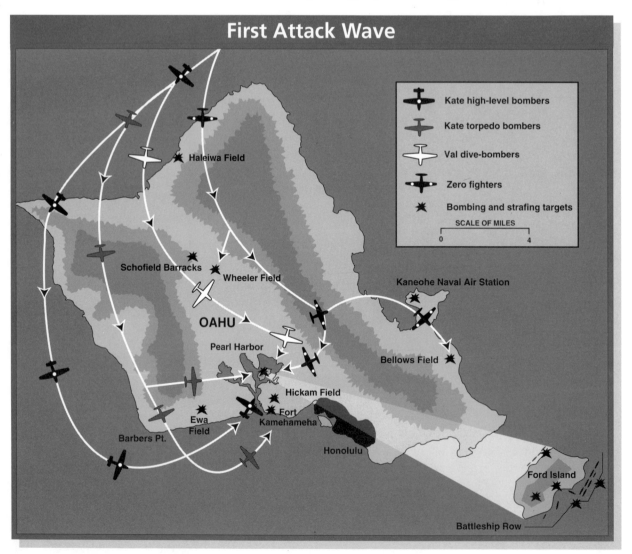

First Attack Wave

Kate high-level bombers

Kate torpedo bombers

Val dive-bombers

Zero fighters

Bombing and strafing targets

SCALE OF MILES

0   4

Haleiwa Field

Schofield Barracks

Wheeler Field

Kaneohe Naval Air Station

OAHU

Pearl Harbor

Bellows Field

Hickam Field

Ewa Field

Fort Kamehameha

Barbers Pt.

Honolulu

Ford Island

Battleship Row

Kimmel rushed outside and watched the planes fly over. "I knew right away that something terrible was going on," he said later, "that this was not a casual raid by just a few stray planes. The sky was full of the enemy." Looking toward Battleship Row, he saw "the *Arizona* lift out of the water, then sink back down—way down."

At 0800, five minutes after the attack began, Kimmel radioed Washington, Admiral Stark, and all the forces at sea: AIR RAID ON PEARL HARBOR. THIS IS NO DRILL.

While Kimmel informed Washington and others of the Japanese attack, Commander Jesse L. Kenworthy, *Oklahoma*'s executive officer and senior officer aboard, ordered his men to abandon ship. He instructed the crew "to leave over the star-

(Top) Clouds of smoke engulf the battleship West Virginia, *which incurred six hits by Japanese torpedoes. Here, a small navy craft helps rescue crewmen trapped aboard the blazing ship. (Above) The waters of Pearl Harbor were filled with debris from damaged and submerged vessels (pictured) following the attack.*

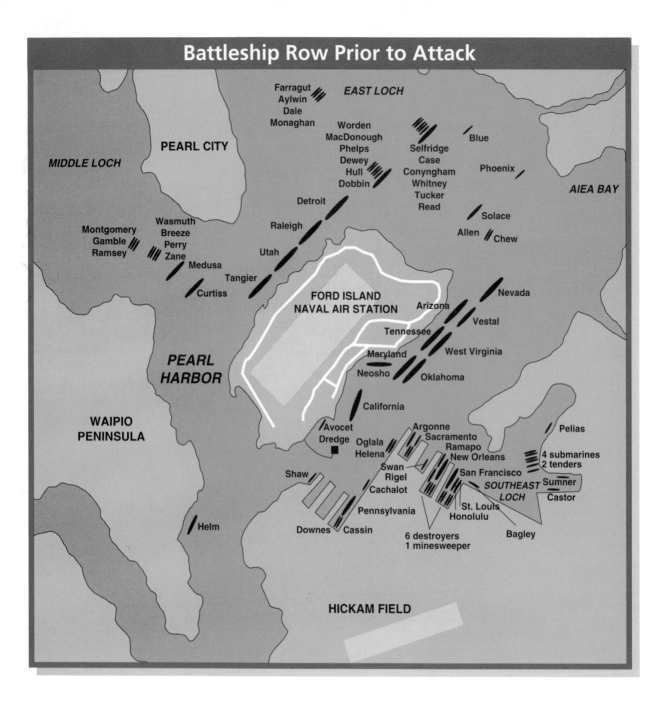

Battleship Row Prior to Attack

EAST LOCH

Farragut
Aylwin
Dale
Monaghan

Worden
MacDonough
Phelps
Dewey
Hull
Dobbin

Blue

Selfridge
Case
Conyngham
Whitney
Tucker
Read

Phoenix

PEARL CITY

MIDDLE LOCH

AIEA BAY

Detroit

Raleigh

Solace

Allen   Chew

Montgomery
Gamble
Ramsey

Wasmuth
Breeze
Perry
Zane

Utah

Medusa

Tangier

Curtiss

FORD ISLAND
NAVAL AIR STATION

Nevada

Arizona

Vestal

Tennessee

West Virginia

Maryland

PEARL
HARBOR

Neosho

Oklahoma

California

WAIPIO
PENINSULA

Avocet
Dredge

Oglala
Helena

Argonne
Sacramento
Ramapo
New Orleans

Pelias

4 submarines
2 tenders

Swan
Rigel
Cachalot

San Francisco

SOUTHEAST
LOCH

Sumner

Castor

Shaw

Pennsylvania

St. Louis
Honolulu

Helm

Downes   Cassin

6 destroyers
1 minesweeper

Bagley

HICKAM FIELD

board side and to work and climb over the ship's side out onto
the bottom as it rolled over." *Oklahoma* heeled over to port and
capsized at 0805.

Arizona took two torpedoes, one of which whizzed right un-
der the repair ship *Vestal*. As described by Chief Boilermaker
John Crawford, the first torpedo "blew the bottom out of *Ari-
zona*." From a vantage point behind *Oklahoma*'s antiroll keel,
First Class Boatswain's Mate Howard C. French looked straight at
Arizona when it exploded.

There was an awful blast and a terrific concussion, but the force was upward instead of out. The foremast tilted forward, took a crazy angle and the ship went down immediately. I could see parts of bodies in the foremast rigging.

Almost one thousand men perished in that frightful explosion. It was 0810.

Berthed inboard, the more sheltered *Tennessee* and *Maryland* temporarily escaped serious damage, as did *Pennsylvania*,

(Left) The U.S. flag gallantly flies aboard the sinking Arizona. *(Below) Sailors line the decks of* Maryland *(left) to watch as* Oklahoma*'s crew abandons the capsized battleship.*

Fuchida's Horizontal Bombing Run

American gunners reacted quickly to the surprise attack on Pearl Harbor. Commander Mitsuo Fuchida, leader of the first-wave attackers, later described the difficulties that he faced over Battleship Row at about 0800, only five minutes into the action:

> As we closed in, enemy antiaircraft fire began to concentrate on us. Dark gray puffs burst all around. Most of them came from ships' batteries, but land batteries were also active. Suddenly my plane bounced as if struck by a club. When I looked back to see what had happened, my radioman said, "The fuselage is holed and the rudder wire damaged." We were fortunate that the plane was still under control, for it was imperative to fly a steady course as we approached the target. Now it was time for "Ready to release," and I concentrated my attention on the lead plane to note the instant his bomb was dropped. Suddenly a cloud came between the bomb sight and the target, and just as I was thinking that we had already overshot, the lead plane banked slightly and turned right toward Honolulu. We had missed the release point because of the cloud and would have to try again.

Sailors aboard California *are evacuated as the badly listing battleship settles into the waters of Pearl Harbor, shrouded by heavy smoke.*

across the channel in drydock one. But at the northern end of Battleship Row, *Nevada* caught a torpedo on its port side at 0803. And at the southern end, *California*, flagship of the Pacific Fleet battle force, sustained two torpedo hits at 0805. Five minutes later, the flagship lost all power and began listing.

The torpedo attack lasted only a few moments. When it ended, the attackers had sunk or badly damaged five battleships, and had dealt crippling blows to two light cruisers, a minelayer, and a repair ship. The Kates left behind little doubt that their attack indeed had been "no drill."

CHAPTER FIVE

"This Country United"

At 0745, about a dozen Zeros rounded Hawaiiloa Hill and turned toward the nearby Kaneohe Naval Air Station. Three minutes later—and seven minutes before the Japanese air strike began at Pearl Harbor—Aviation Machinist's Mate Third Class Guy C. Avery heard "the sound of a lone plane quite near our house" at Kaneohe. The plane's engine sounded strange to him. He dashed to the window of the bungalow that he and a few squadron mates shared and looked out in time to see "Zeros just beginning to fan out over the heart of the station and opening fire promiscuously." He yelled at once to his still-sleeping mates, "The Japs are here! It's war!" No one took him seriously.

One of his disbelieving mates replied, "Well, don't worry about it, Avery. It'll last only two weeks."

Kaneohe Naval Air Station

Located on the eastern side of Oahu, Kaneohe was the home of Patrol Wing One, with a complement of thirty-six PBY-5 (Catalina) flying boats and a few miscellaneous aircraft. Four PBYs were moored in the bay that morning, according to Kaneohe's commanding officer, Commander Harold M. Martin, "at about a thousand yards apart." The rest of the PBYs, in observance of a sabotage warning issued the day before, "were parked on the [seaplane] ramp except for four which were in No. 1 hangar."

While enjoying Sunday morning coffee at his quarters, Martin saw the Zeros coming "almost head-on," flying at a height of about eight hundred feet. He assumed them to be some of Halsey's planes coming in to land in advance of *Enterprise.*

Martin took a closer look when his thirteen-year-old son David said, "Dad, those planes have red circles on them."

Kaneohe's skipper pulled on his uniform over his blue silk pajamas and zoomed off in his car. By the time he arrived at his command post, "the first plane on the water had begun to burn." The Zeros were only getting started. Before leaving, the fighters destroyed all four PBYs moored in the bay.

At 0815, eighteen more Japanese planes, mostly dive-bombers (Vals), struck the field. The unprepared and under-armed Americans fought back with little effect on the Japanese, but well enough to make their commander proud. "It was re-markable," Martin said. "There was no panic. Everyone went right to work battling back and doing his job."

The second group of attackers devastated the air station, how-ever, and a third group was still to come. Of Kaneohe's thirty-six PBYs, only three on patrol flights escaped unharmed; six were damaged, and the remaining twenty-seven were demolished.

(Below) Japan's battery of Pearl Harbor left hangars and aircraft in shambles. (Below, right) An aerial photograph of the Kaneohe Naval Air Station shows the damage caused by the Japanese raid.

Wheeler Field

At Wheeler Field, in central Oahu—home of the Fourteenth Pursuit Wing—base commander Colonel William J. Flood had just opened the morning paper when he heard "this awful *whang*." He rushed outside to see Japanese planes

> bombing and strafing the base, the planes, the officers' quarters, and even the golf course. I could even see some of the Japanese pilots lean out of their planes and smile as they zoomed by. They were that damn low—just a few feet above the ground really, not much higher than a man's head. Hell, I could even see the gold in their teeth.

The Fourteenth Pursuit Wing held full responsibility for the island's aerial defense. There were 140 fighters in the wing: 87 fairly modern P-40s, 35 of which were out of commission; 39 obsolete P-36s, and 14 ancient P-26s, of which 20 and 10, respectively, were flyable. The Forty-fourth and Forty-seventh Pursuit Squadrons were detached temporarily to nearby Bellows Field

(Above) Extensive bombing and strafing by Japanese aircraft devastated Wheeler Field. (Below, left) The wreckage of a P-40 fighter at Bellows Field remains as evidence of the Japanese attack.

Bellows Field

American aircraft attempting to take off from Bellows Field became easy prey for Japanese Zeros led by Lieutenant Fusata Iida. Base commander Lieutenant Colonel Leonard Weddington looked on in helpless frustration as two P-40s fell victim to the Zeros. He described their plight:

I personally watched, wondering what would happen if the pilot [of the first P-40] was hit while taxiing, whether the airplane would just go on off, over the island, or whether he would die there, or whether he would groundloop, or what would happen. . . . Six different airplanes made passes at him and seemingly never hit him, but when he got on the runway and started to take off, they got right square behind him, and just as he got off, shot him down in flames; and he was turning, trying to give them a bad target, and crashed into the beach and burned there.

The other one that they shot down taking off, I did not see take off, because there were some of them making passes at the position I was in at the time, and I ducked. I had seen him taxiing down, however. They shot him down in the same manner, except that he was not so badly shot up, landed in the water about three quarters of a mile to a mile down the beach, and swam ashore. He was not killed.

and Haleiwa Field to the north for gunnery practice. Most of the P-40s at Wheeler were lined up on the airstrip wingtip to wingtip, to guard against potential sabotage attempts. Not one fighter made it aloft that morning.

Twenty-five Vals from *Zuikaku*, led by Lieutenant Akira Sakamoto, bombed Wheeler first at 0755. Two American machine gunners fired back valiantly, but without effect.

A wave of Lieutenant Kiyokuma Okajima's Fourth Air Control Group Zeros, off *Hiryu*, followed with a strafing attack. When fighter pilot First Petty Officer Kazuo Muranaka arrived, he saw "flashes of fire caused by hits on hangars. . . . Wheeler air base was already a sea of fire."

The air over Wheeler Field was so crowded that Okajima and his Zeros soon departed for Ewa, the marine airfield west of Pearl Harbor. The Vals lingered at Wheeler long enough to demolish the hangars, post exchange, and enlisted men's barracks, killing several hundred airmen instantly and seriously wounding many more. When the bombers left, one half of Wheeler's fighters lay in smoking ruins. "It was a pitiful, unholy mess," Colonel Flood said.

Hickam Field

A similar attack commenced on Hickam Field, just east of Pearl Harbor, at 0755. The headquarters of the Hawaiian Air Force resided at Hickam, as did the Eighteenth Bombardment Wing. The bomber wing's twelve B-17s, thirty-two B-18s, and thirteen A-20s represented the island's greatest threat for striking back against Nagumo's *Kido Butai*. Accordingly, the Japanese lashed Hickam with the full force of fighter, dive-bomber, and high-level bomber attacks.

The first Japanese attack on Hickam came from two groups of dive-bombers from *Shokaku*, twenty-six in all, whose assigned mission was "to dive-bomb carriers in the harbor and, if they are not there, to attack Hickam air base" and then strafe until relieved by "friendly fighters." In the absence of any "carriers in the harbor," Lieutenant Iwakichi Mifuku and his squadron mates off *Shokaku* dive-bombed Hickam's hangars and "then strafed parked planes on the base."

Twenty-four men were caught in the bombing and strafing attack while preparing several B-18s for a training flight. Bomb blasts and machine-gun fire killed twenty-two and "cut the legs off the other two."

Lieutenant Howard F. Cooper, commander of Headquarters Squadron, Seventeenth Air Base Group, was awakened by exploding bombs. "Dive bombers were tearing the place to pieces, blasting everything."

Hickam Field, home to the Hawaiian Air Force and the Eighteenth Bombardment Wing, before the attack on Pearl Harbor. Japanese aces quickly demolished hangars and aircraft with bombs and strafing fire.

Major Landon's twelve B-17s began arriving from the mainland at 0815, in the midst of flame and fury. A group of planes flew toward his formation from the south as if to greet him. Landon thought at first that they were friendly. Then they peeled over, revealing the bright red balls of the rising-sun emblem on their wings and attacked his bombers with all guns blazing. Someone shouted over the intercom, "Damn it, those are Japs!"

By some miracle, all twelve B-17s landed intact. Two landed at Haleiwa, one at Wheeler, another at Bellows, seven at Hickam, and one, the twelfth, pancaked down on Kahuku golf course. Once down, however, strafing fire destroyed one and badly damaged three others. But they had made it to their destination, albeit somewhat worse for the wear.

The Japanese attackers caught Hickam by complete surprise, just as they had surprised the fleet in Pearl Harbor. They knocked out more than half of the field's aircraft, trashed hangars, and destroyed many other important buildings. When the raiders finally turned away, they left behind 138 dead and missing Americans and 336 wounded. Of all the army bases, Hickam took the worst pounding that morning.

(Below) Under siege by Japanese fighters, this B-17 was forced to make a crash landing at Bellows Field. (Below, right) An aircraft hangar at Hickam Field stands in ruins after being pounded by Japanese bombs.

"My God, What a Sight!"

Of forty-eight planes lined up at Ewa Field on December 7, 1941, forty-seven never got off the ground. When the Japanese struck the marine air station that Sunday morning, Private First Class Bob Wells, USMC, and some comrades took cover in the walk-in refrigerators behind the mess hall. Wells later described what he saw right after emerging from the makeshift shelter to Henry Berry, author of *"This Is No Drill!"*:

My God, what a sight! We had forty-eight planes of different types lined up. The Japanese had done a number on all of them.

The two of us [Wells and another marine] each picked up bolt-action Springfield rifles. A jeep drove by with loaded bandoleers [ammunition belts] in it. A sergeant in the jeep was tossing out these bandoleers. We each caught one and went over to where they were building a new swimming pool. There was a bulldozer parked at the site. Using it for cover, we started shooting our rifles at the Japanese planes as they flew by. I don't think we hit anything, but we could let off some steam.

Then, out of nowhere, two American planes appeared. I later found out they were piloted by two Army men named Welch and Taylor.

Boy, did they tear into those Japanese planes! I saw two go down. There might have been more.

. . . but they [the Japanese] surely knocked the American airfields to pieces. Not only Ewa, but also Wheeler, Bellows, and Hickam. Just about every place we had planes was devastated.

Kathleen Bruns Cooper, nineteen-year-old daughter of a navy captain and newly married to a submarine officer, watched the attack on Hickam from her parents' neighborhood that overlooked the field. She recalled that the field looked "like a great sea of flame about a mile long." Cooper felt so outraged that she added, "If a Japanese pilot had walked in the house [right then], I would have tried to kill him." No one doubted her.

Ewa Field

Across the bay from Hickam, twenty-one Japanese fighters roared around the Waianae Range northwest of Pearl Harbor and began shooting up the marine air station at Ewa Field at 0755. The Zeros made pass after pass. They flew as low as twenty feet off the ground, raking the personnel of Marine Aircraft Group Twenty-one (MAG-21) with incendiary, explosive, and armor-piercing rounds from 7.7-millimeter machine guns and 20-

millimeter cannons. The Zeros concentrated their attack on the tactical aircraft lined up on the airstrip, destroying forty-seven of forty-eight fighter planes in the first fifteen minutes.

With their flyable aircraft rendered useless by the strafing attackers and without benefit of antiaircraft defenses, the marines answered the marauders with their only available means: rifles and .30-caliber machine guns stripped from wrecked planes. A few marines added Thompson submachine guns to the woeful mix.

After wiping out the marine fighters, the Zeros focused their attention on aircraft undergoing repair and personnel. A group of Vals joined the attack at 0835 and bombed hangars and other ground facilities. Twelve more Japanese planes struck Ewa for a third time between 0900 and 0930. But base and MAG-21 commander Lieutenant Colonel Claude A. Larkin described their final assault as "light and ineffectual."

Zero pilot Lieutenant Yoshio Shiga would long remember his last glimpse of the field as he turned his Zero away from Ewa to return to *Kaga*. Years later he still recalled the image of "a gallant

Kido Butai *severely crippled U.S. forces stationed at Pearl Harbor. (Below) American soldiers maintain a careful watch for Japanese raiders looming on the horizon.*

soldier on the ground attempting to shoot us with his pistol, to whom I paid a good respect." The "gallant soldier" was marine Private First Class Mel Thompson, an angry sentry at Ewa's main gate, cranking off rounds from his .45. His act typified the fearless futility that American defenders displayed that morning.

Haleiwa Field

Only a handful of American fighter pilots made it off the ground to engage the enemy over Oahu that Sunday morning. Most notable among them were Second Lieutenants George S. Welch and Kenneth Taylor of the Forty-seventh Pursuit Squadron, temporarily assigned to Haleiwa Field on Oahu's northern shore. Except for one brief strafing pass on the tiny training field, the Japanese pilots had pretty much ignored Haleiwa in favor of choicer targets farther south. In the absence of the base commander and pilots standing by at Haleiwa on Sunday morning, the duty officer ordered a neat line of P-40s on the airstrip to be disbursed. Ignoring the duty officer's orders, Welch and Taylor boarded P-40s and zoomed aloft at 0820. The two pilots promptly found themselves engaged, outnumbered, and fighting to stay alive.

Taylor later described the action:

I made a nice turn out into them and got in a string of six or eight planes. I don't know how many there were. . . . I was on one's tail as we went over Waialua, firing at the one next to me, and there was one following firing at me, and I pulled out. I don't know what happened to the other plane. Lieutenant Welch, I think, shot the other man down.

Second Lieutenants Kenneth Taylor (third from left) and George S. Welch (fourth from left) disobeyed orders to disburse and in the process shot down seven enemy planes between them.

Welch confirmed the kill. "We took off directly into them and shot some down. I shot down one right on Lieutenant Taylor's tail."

The two lieutenants survived the uneven battle to refuel and return to action twice during the Japanese attack. By morning's end, the two pilots had shot down seven enemy planes between them. Welch was recommended for the Medal of Honor but received only the Distinguished Flying Cross because he had disobeyed orders.

At least a dozen fighter pilots from Haleiwa and Wheeler Fields made it into the air that morning, collectively accounting for ten confirmed kills and an undetermined number of probables. Two American pilots were killed in the course of these actions.

A Moment of History

In his acclaimed novel *From Here to Eternity*, writer James Jones described Japan's attack on Schofield Barracks in vivid detail. Jones based his fictional account on his own experiences as a company clerk in the Twenty-seventh Infantry Regiment. For the author, December 7, 1941, began much like any other Sunday:

At Schofield Barracks in the infantry quadrangles, those of us who were up were at breakfast. On Sunday morning in those days there was a bonus ration of a half-pint of milk, to go with your eggs or pancakes and syrup, also Sunday specials. Most of us were more concerned with getting and holding onto our half-pints of milk than with listening to the explosions that began rumbling up toward us from Wheeler Field two miles away. "They doing some blasting?" some old-timer said through a mouthful of pancakes. It was not till the first low-flying fighter came skidding, whammering low overhead with his MGs [machine guns] going that we ran outside, still clutching our half-pints of milk to keep them from being stolen, aware with a sudden sense of awe that we were seeing and acting in a genuine moment of history.

Welch (left) and Taylor (right) were each awarded the Distinguished Flying Cross for their valiant efforts during the Japanese assault.

Schofield Barracks

The Ninety-eighth Coast Artillery Regiment was charged with the antiaircraft defense at Schofield Barracks, primarily an army infantry installation adjacent to Wheeler Field. Two soldiers assigned to communications duties with the regiment provided some antiaircraft defense of their own that morning but not in the conventional manner.

At 0825, Lieutenant Stephen G. Saltzman heard "what sounded like two planes pulling out of a dive over Kam [Kamehameha] Highway." Saltzman grabbed a BAR (Browning automatic rifle) and "a couple of clips of ammunition" from a nearby soldier in the barracks and rushed outside. Sergeant Lowell V. Klatt also snatched a BAR and ammo and followed the lieutenant's lead. Two Vals roared out of Kolekole Pass and headed straight at them. Both men dropped to their knees, just as the first Val "opened up with his four machine guns." The lieutenant was "too mad to be scared" and emptied his clip at the onrushing dive bombers, as did the cool-headed sergeant.

The first plane swerved to the left and flew off safely; the second flashed by overhead and out of sight behind a building. In only "two seconds at the most," they heard "this crash and a blast," Klatt recalled. He and Saltzman ran to the crash scene and found two dead airmen. The Japanese likely had been killed on impact, because their badly burned bodies "were just all crashed down in the cockpit."

Fallen Honor

While fortune favored most of Japan's airmen, the ten crew members of the Imperial Navy's five midget submarines—the Special Attack Unit—fared far less well. Their mission was to penetrate Pearl Harbor before dawn on December 7 and lie in wait on the ocean floor for the aerial attack to begin. When Nagumo's planes arrived overhead, the midget submarines would strike from below, by torpedoing capital ships or the best targets available. The scenario did not play out that way.

The Americans sunk four of the tiny submarines and captured the fifth. Not one midget submarine scored a hit at Pearl Harbor. The twenty-five large submarines fanned out south of the harbor entrance did little more than observe the action. (The submarine *I-70* was sunk in Hawaiian waters on December 10.)

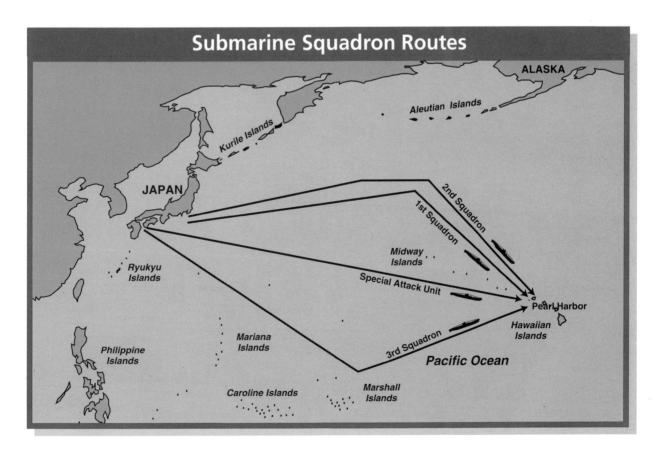

Perhaps the most determined submariners were Ensign Kazuo Sakamaki and Petty Officer Second Class Kiyoshi Inagaki. Before leaving *I-24*, their parent submarine, they discovered a faulty compass on their midget craft. It would be impossible to reach their destination without a properly functioning compass. When asked by *I-24*'s captain what he wanted to do, Sakamaki replied, "On to Pearl Harbor!" Inagaki concurred.

But they ran afoul of reefs three times and failed to reach Pearl Harbor. Hung up on a reef for the third time, they tried to blow up their craft with an explosive charge and swim for shore. Inagaki drowned in the attempt, the charge failed to explode, and Sakamaki passed out from exhaustion and was washed ashore. When he revived, Sakamaki found himself in the custody of Sergeant David M. Akui. Sakamaki had just claimed the dubious honor of becoming the first prisoner captured by the United States in World War II. His submarine was later towed ashore intact by a bulldozer.

While being questioned, Sakamaki complained to his captors that his "honor as a soldier has fallen to the ground," because he had allowed himself to be captured. He then pleaded, "Please do not advise Japan about this. Please kill me." They did not. Japanese accounts later ignored Sakamaki's capture and heralded the heroic deeds of the midget submariners.

A Japanese midget submarine is recovered from its shallow grave in the waters off Pearl Harbor. The sailors who helped to raise the resting sub stand triumphantly on the craft's hull.

A Cold Reception

While American casualties poured into the Pearl Harbor Navy Yard dispensary, and hospitals and temporary hospitals throughout the island, President Roosevelt called Cordell Hull at 1405 that afternoon (0835 in Hawaii) to inform him of Admiral Kimmel's message about the Japanese attack. Officials in Washington still found it hard to believe that the Japanese would dare to attack Pearl Harbor.

Meanwhile, Ambassador Nomura and Special Envoy Kurusu had arrived at Hull's office and were waiting outside to deliver Tokyo's fourteen-part reply to America's peace proposals. (Delivery of the diplomatic note, originally scheduled for 1300 on December 7, had been delayed because of the extra time required for decoding the lengthy document.) Roosevelt instructed Hull to receive the Japanese diplomats "but to mention nothing about Pearl Harbor." Hull was only "to receive their reply formally and coolly and bow them out."

At 1420 Hull "received them coldly and did not ask them to sit down." Nomura handed Hull the note, with apologies for not delivering the note at one o'clock. Hull wanted to know "why he had specified one o'clock." Nomura answered "that he did not know but that that was his instruction." Hull emphasized "that anyway he was receiving the message at two o'clock." The secretary clearly wanted to etch the time in the minds of Nomura and Kurusu.

The secretary of state scanned the document, then fixed an icy stare on Nomura and said:

> I must say that in all my conversations with you in the last nine months, I have never uttered one word of untruth. This is borne out absolutely by the record. In all my fifty years of public service I have never seen a document that was more crowded with infamous falsehoods and distortions—infamous falsehoods and distortions on a scale so huge that I have never imagined until today that any Government on this planet was capable of uttering them.

The secretary denied any response, merely nodding toward the door. The two diplomats walked out of Hull's office with bowed heads.

Nomura added a brief entry to his diary later that day: "The report of our surprise attack against Hawaii reached my ears when I returned home from the state department; *this might have reached Hull's ears during our conversation*" (Nomura's italics).

While Special Envoy Kurusu and Ambassador Nomura (above) were waiting to deliver a response regarding the American peace proposal, Secretary of State Hull (below) was informed of Japan's strike on Pearl Harbor.

The Narrow Line

"We learned in Honolulu that Sunday how narrow the dividing line is between the soldier and civilian in wartime," wrote Blake Clark, an associate professor of English at the University of Hawaii. "Soon after the bombing started, a call came into the headquarters of the Hawaii Medical Association. The voice just said: 'Pearl Harbor! Ambulances! For God's sake, hurry!'" The professor went on to describe how the call was answered:

Within twenty minutes doctors and volunteer workers had stripped the insides of more than 100 delivery trucks of every description, equipped them neatly with previously prepared stretcher frames and were speeding to the scene of action.

Women of the Motor Corps, in every available car, were carrying men to Pearl Harbor. The three-lane highway was an inferno. Army trucks, official and unofficial emergency wagons, ambulances, Red Cross cars and hundreds of taxis rushing officers and men to their battle stations screamed up and down the six-mile road. The Motor Corps women were equal to the task.

The Army wounded were taken to Tripler Army Hospital. Surgeon [Colonel Edgar] King put in an emergency call for surgical teams to the doctors of Honolulu. Then occurred one of life's breathtaking coincidences. At that very moment, about fifty Honolulu doctors were listening to a lecture on war surgery delivered by Dr. John J. Moorhead of New York. The audience departed in a group for Tripler.

It had, of course, as Nomura learned later. The suddenness of Japan's attack both shocked and surprised him. Secretary of War Henry L. Stimson reacted somewhat differently to the news.

When the news first came that Japan had attacked us, my first feeling was of relief that the indecision was over and a crisis had come in a way which would unite our people. This continued to be my dominant feeling in spite of the news of catastrophes which quickly developed. For I feel that this country united has practically nothing to fear while the apathy and divisions stirred up by unpatriotic men have been hitherto very discouraging.

CHAPTER SIX

An End and a Beginning

Lieutenant Commander Shigekazu Shimazaki's second attack wave—fifty-four Kate high-level bombers, seventy-seven Val dive-bombers, and thirty-six Zero fighters—arrived over Oahu at about 0840. Twenty-seven Kates were assigned to a second pass at Hickam Field; the remaining twenty-seven were to pound Ford Island again. All seventy-seven Vals were to concentrate on destroying as many ships as possible. In the meantime, the Zeros would sweep the air clear of enemy opposition and execute strafing attacks on Wheeler Field and Kaneohe.

When the original attackers exhausted their ordnance and turned northward to return to *Kido Butai*, their leader, Commander Mitsuo Fuchida, remained behind for a few minutes to direct the second-wave pilots. Fuchida soon heard Shimazaki's attack order *"To, To, To!"* and checked the time. It was 0855.

The second wave would not enjoy the ideal attack conditions born of surprise and an unsuspecting enemy, as had the first wave about an hour earlier. Flame and smoke now shrouded targets and interfered with bombing accuracy. And antiaircraft fire laced the air with explosive puffs of flying steel. But the fate of Pearl Harbor and its sur-

A Kate high-level bomber takes off from a Japanese aircraft carrier. During the second attack wave, fifty-four Kates were employed to continue assaults on Hickam Field and Ford Island.

Smoke from burning ships filled the skies over Pearl Harbor, obscuring targets for Japan's second attack wave.

rounding military installations had already been decided. By then, American defenses had been rendered incapable of deterring the second-wave airmen from the efficient completion of their tasks. Hundreds of Americans would die trying, however, as testament to Japanese treachery and American courage and determination.

Monaghan Sinks Sub

A moment before Shimazaki deployed his second wave, the U.S. destroyer *Monaghan* was cruising on a southwesterly course between Pearl City and Ford Island, heading toward the open sea. With Pearl Harbor under heavy attack, Lieutenant Commander William P. Burford, *Monaghan*'s skipper, wanted "to get out of that damn harbor as fast as possible." At 0839, a message from the seaplane tender *Curtiss* warned of a submarine sighting. Burford refused to believe that an enemy submarine could navigate in Pearl Harbor's shallow waters. When his signalman verified the message, Burford said, "Well, *Curtiss* must be crazy."

Then a crew member pointed off the starboard bow and said, "That may be so, Captain, but what is that down there?"

Burford looked off to the right about twelve hundred yards and spotted "an over and under shotgun barrel looking up" at him. (He was looking at the twin torpedo ports of a midget submarine.) "I don't know what the hell it is," he told his companions on the bridge, "but it shouldn't be there." He ordered full-ahead speed and set a course for ramming the undersea intruder.

"It was a hectic few minutes," Burford related afterward.

There was that sub coming directly at me, and I at him, and all that speed, and the firing by others, and a number of ships out ahead of me in restricted maneuvering space, and all the Japanese air attack behind us and our antiaircraft fire, their planes—God, a lot was going on in just a few minutes of time.

At 0840, the submarine "commenced surfacing in damaged condition and was hit directly with both 5-inch and .50 caliber shells" from *Curtiss*. The submarine displayed a "5-inch shell hole

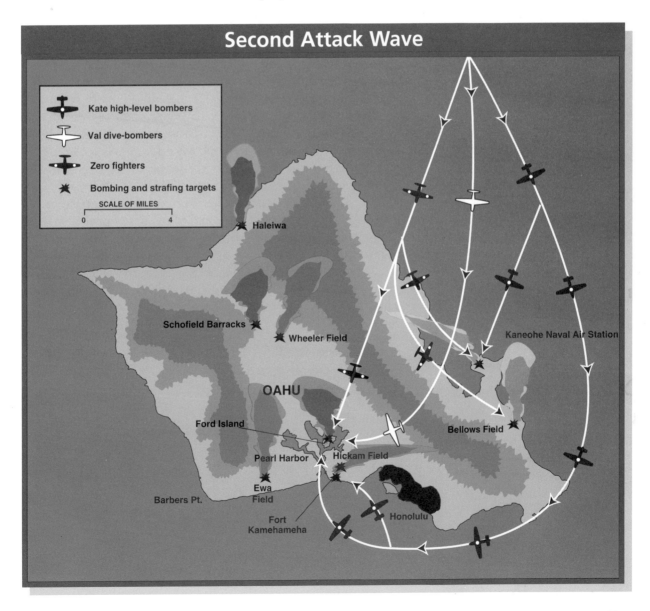

A "Most Noticeable" Strike

The battleship *Nevada* tried valiantly to flee Pearl Harbor and escape to the open sea. But several Japanese bombs ended *Nevada's* flight in midchannel. Ensign John L. Landreth recalled near misses on the battlewagon and the "most noticeable" strike, which went through the gunfire directory platform:

> One plane came in and dropped one short. We could see that one go short and land in the water. Another one came in a little too far to the left and dropped it over us, and the third one came in right between these, and we could see before he did that it was going to be fairly close, and when he dropped it the bomb came right directly at our directory, and we were certain it was going to hit us. It hit about a foot from the director and went through the director platform, went through the navigation bridge deck, went through the signal bridge and down into the captain's cabin and exploded somewhere probably below the captain's cabin, caused great damage in personnel in casement 4 and casement 6, just went below and was stopped by the third deck, armor deck.

through the conning tower, which killed the captain. He was blown into a mass of crumpled steel."

The submarine fired two torpedoes at *Monaghan* and missed with both. The destroyer struck the submarine with a glancing blow and dumped two depth charges on it as *Monaghan* sliced on past. Burford observed that the depth charges "just tore hell out of the [submarine's] bow." The submarine sank, and with a full head of steam, *Monaghan* safely cleared the harbor at 0908.

Nevada Ordered Aground

At about 0855, just before the second-wave bombers arrived, *Nevada* got under way, despite severe torpedo and bomb damage incurred during the first attack. Lieutenant Commander Francis Thomas, the senior officer aboard *Nevada*, wanted to move the crippled battleship away from *Arizona's* searing heat and flame. Chief Quartermaster Robert Sedberry's steady hand guided *Nevada* through the narrow channel, past its burning neighbor, and on by the overturned *Oklahoma*, "another terrifying and shocking sight." Sedberry threaded the bulky vessel through a narrow gap formed by the badly listing *Oglala* and the dredge *Turbine*. Moving smoothly toward the harbor mouth and the comparative safety of the open sea, *Nevada* ran out of luck.

Circling overhead, Commander Fuchida recognized a splendid opportunity to deal a double blow to the Pacific Fleet. If his airmen could sink *Nevada* at the entrance to the channel, the sunken vessel would bottle up the harbor and cancel Pearl Harbor's usefulness as a major operating base for perhaps months to come. *Nevada* had just drawn abreast of the flaming floating dry dock, adjacent to Hospital Point, when a swarm of Egusa's dive-bombers struck at 0907. Five bombs exploded in *Nevada's* superstructure and bow.

The capsized Oklahoma *reposes in the waters of Pearl Harbor. Sailors had to navigate their way around overturned and burning ships in the narrow channel during the attack.*

With his ship listing badly and still under attack, Thomas ordered Sedberry to run *Nevada* aground at Hospital Point at 0910. The vital channel would remain open.

Arizona Abandoned

Lieutenant Commander Samuel G. Fuqua had pulled head-of-department duty aboard *Arizona* on December 6. As damage control officer, he carried responsibility for "the watertight integrity of the ship and to keep it afloat in case of damage in battle." When *Arizona*'s forward ammunition magazine exploded at 0810 the next morning, killing Captain Franklin Van Valkenburgh, *Arizona*'s skipper, and Rear Admiral Isaac C. Kidd, First Battleship Division commander, Fuqua suddenly found himself senior officer in charge.

Just prior to the huge blast that killed more than a thousand men in one horrible instant, Fuqua and his damage control crew had been fighting fires, trying "to keep the fire back by dipping water from the side in buckets and by the use of CO_2 extinguisher." Following the blast, with the ship devastated beyond hope of saving, he directed his efforts toward evacuating the

(Above, left) The Americans run the badly damaged Nevada *aground at Hospital Point to keep the entrance to Pearl Harbor open. (Above) A huge column of smoke swells above* Arizona *as the ship's ammunition magazine explodes.*

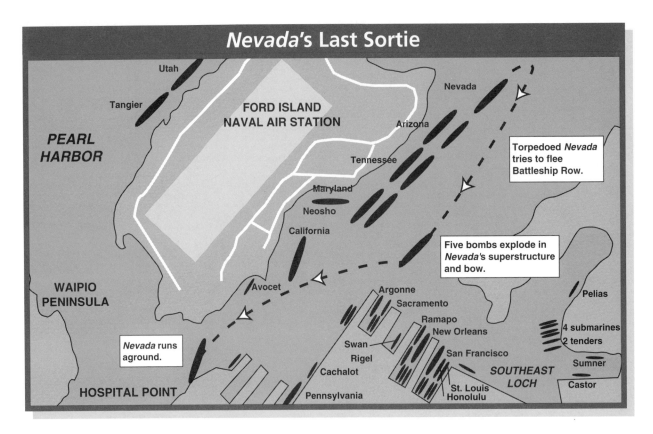

Nevada's Last Sortie

Utah

Tangier

FORD ISLAND NAVAL AIR STATION

PEARL HARBOR

Nevada

Arizona

Tennessee

Maryland

Neosho

California

Torpedoed *Nevada* tries to flee Battleship Row.

WAIPIO PENINSULA

Avocet

Argonne

Sacramento

Ramapo

New Orleans

Pelias

Five bombs explode in *Nevada*'s superstructure and bow.

Swan

Rigel

Cachalot

San Francisco

4 submarines
2 tenders

Sumner

***Nevada* runs aground.**

SOUTHEAST LOCH

HOSPITAL POINT

Pennsylvania

St. Louis
Honolulu

Castor

wounded. For almost an hour, Fuqua stood fast in the face of machine-gun fire and advancing flame and searing heat, overseeing the removal of burned and mangled crew members.

By his own count, he personally evacuated more than seventy men. His devotion to ship and shipmates served as an inspiration to all the living still aboard and fighting for survival.

Aviation Machinist's Mate Donald "Turkey" Graham spoke for many when he later said, "It seemed like the men painfully burned, shocked and dazed, became inspired and took things in stride, seeing Mr. Fuqua, so unconcerned about the bombing and strafing."

One of the last sailors to go over the side asked Fuqua when he intended to swim to shore. "When the Japs leave," he replied. At about 0900, as nearly as Fuqua could later recall (although it was probably earlier), he reluctantly or-

Arizona crewmen fought flames and searing heat as they evacuated the sinking ship.

dered abandon ship. His grace under pressure earned him the Medal of Honor and the undying gratitude of untold shipmates.

Vows to Keep

Individual acts of valor occurred as regularly as heartbeats at Pearl Harbor. And, as keenly evidenced by the sacrifices of Lieutenants Fusata Iida and Mimori Suzuki, courage knew no sides.

Commencing at approximately 0900, Iida led nine Third Air Control Group fighters from *Soryu* in a third attack on Kaneohe Naval Air Station. He found the field already under attack by nine of Shimizaki's high-level bombers. One of their bombs had just struck a hangar with ammunition stores, igniting the ordnance and causing the greatest loss of life at the station. Iida's Zeros swept in from the east, across the distinctive line of cliffs behind Kaneohe known as the *pali*, and started strafing everything that moved and a lot that did not.

Iida's fighter was hit by ground fire and began streaming fuel as he climbed out of the field to rejoin his squadron mates. Signaling them northward to return to their carrier, he pointed first at himself and then at the ground. His pilots understood. Iida then turned back toward the field and plunged earthward, intent upon keeping his vow to crash-dive into an enemy target rather than bail out. But the gallant pilot missed any important targets and crashed harmlessly into a hillside.

Three Japanese attacks on Kaneohe left the field in shambles and all but three American aircraft were destroyed or severely damaged. The success of the attacks was blemished only by the loss of Iida and one other pilot who crashed into Kailua Bay. A third Japanese pilot crashed farther to the west at about the same time.

At 0905, antiaircraft fire from the seaplane tender *Curtiss*, the cruiser *Raleigh*, and probably other ships, struck Lieutenant Mimori Suzuki's Val during an attack on ships northwest of Ford Island. His Val, according to *Curtiss*'s log, "was hit badly and burst into flames." Suzuki then crashed—deliberately, according to observers—into *Curtiss*'s No. 1 crane, "where it burned completely." Another vow kept.

Lucky Scouts

Somewhere around 0900, six SBDs from *Enterprise* arrived at Ewa, between attacks on the marine air base. "They came down in the normal method of identification and procedure and came to our field," according to base commander Larkin, "and we took them aboard." He ordered them back in the air with all due haste. The SBDs proceeded from Ewa to Ford Island and received a hot welcome.

Iida's End

At Kaneohe Naval Air Station, Aviation Machinist's Mate Third Class Guy C. Avery witnessed Lieutenant Fusata Iida's fatal plunge into a nearby hillside. The Japanese fighter pilot had apparently honored an earlier vow to crash-dive into an American target should his Zero become disabled. Avery grimly recollected the end of Iida's story:

> Lieutenant Iida's . . . body was taken up in a galvanized iron garbage can, not entirely out of disrespect—although heaven knows we despised him and his kind to the limit that day—but because we had no more suitable facility at hand. . . . The garbage can with its revolting contents was left on the front walk outside the sick bay entrance for the remainder of the day. We had sixteen of our own corpses awaiting care in the improvised morgue, and besides, there was nothing more that could be done for him then. Many of our own men were very indignant because he was given a dignified military funeral and interment along with those Americans who died that tragic day.

At about 0930 on December 7, Storekeeper Third Class Jack Rogo hurried from the Pearl Harbor infirmary to his official battle station on the roof of the supply department building, overlooking the navy yard. The view spread out below him would become forever etched in his memory. Twenty years later, he recalled:

The panoramic view of Pearl Harbor was breathtaking. . . . To my right, across the channel was the USS *Shaw* all twisted in her dry dock. To my right on Ford Island lay the wreckage of our seaplane hangars with all of their windows blown out, and our seaplanes in a mass of twisted wreckage. Ahead of me the USS *Nevada*, listing, was steaming out to sea. She never made it and was beached at the mouth of the main channel. To my left was Battleship Row. I cannot remember the names or the positions of the ships now, but they were all damaged, listing, sunk, and some turned bottom up. Behind me, looking across Ford Island, I could see the bottom of the USS *Utah* rising from the water and the damaged fantail of the USS *Curtiss*.

Ensign Cleo Dobson tried to land at Ford with what looked to him like every gun on the island shooting at him. He barely made it down through a storm of tracers and bursting pom-pom shells. Commanders Young and Nichol, bearing Admiral Halsey's message to Admiral Kimmel, experienced similar landing difficulties. Nichol recalled that they "went through the damnest amount of anti-aircraft fire and bullet fire we had ever seen, before or since, and finally got in to the field at Ford Island."

This pair of SBDs was among the lucky ones from *Enterprise*. Of eighteen scouts sent to Pearl Harbor in advance of Halsey's task force, five fell to Zeros or "friendly" antiaircraft fire.

"Praise the Lord and Pass the Ammunition!"

Luck deserted *Pennsylvania* when one of Egusa's dive-bombers discovered the battleship in drydock one and scored a direct hit at 0902. Five minutes later, a high-level bomber landed another direct hit at the starboard side of the boat deck, killing two officers and eleven enlisted men. The blast also left thirty-eight wounded, fourteen missing, and two unidentified bodies.

Fire broke out on *Pennsylvania* and spread to two destroyers at the dock's head. According to *Pennsylvania's* log, "Fire engulfed both USS CASSIN and USS DOWNES." They both had to be abandoned. By 0930, the fires had set off magazines and exploded torpedo warheads on the two destroyers. *Cassin* then rolled over against the stricken *Downes*, both vessels torn and gutted almost beyond recognition.

Three hundred yards west of *Pennsylvania*, the destroyer *Shaw* took three bomb hits between 0900 and 0930, while berthed with the tug *Sotoyomo* in the navy yard's floating drydock two. Five more bombs struck the dock itself, setting it ablaze, and ripping off its entire bow. The flames spread out of control, igniting *Shaw's* forward ammunition magazine and rocking the harbor with the most spectacular explosion of the morning. "I couldn't describe it," said an ensign who observed the blast from the repair ship *Vestal*. "It was just a great big whoof!"

Another group of dive-bombers attacked *Curtiss* at 0912. Three bombs missed, but the fourth bomb struck the starboard side of the tender's boat deck, killing twenty-one crew members and demolishing everything within a thirty-foot radius of the blast. But *Curtiss's* gunners fought back, firing at high-level bombers at 0928. Damage-control shipmates successfully struggled to save the ship.

Amid the smoke and flame, and under fierce and furious dive-bombing and machine-gunning attacks, the destroyers *Dale* and *Blue* managed to clear the harbor at 0907 and 0910, respectively, and thus survived to fight another day.

At 0912, a bomb struck twelve feet away from the ammunition ship *Pyro*; the ship was tied up at the ammunition depot in Pearl Harbor's remote West Loch. The bomb pierced the concrete and exploded beneath the pier. Although rocked by the blast, the fully loaded *Pyro* sustained only minor damage. This small miracle enabled a group of marines to transfer antiaircraft ammunition from *Pyro* to a small launch and distribute the much-needed ammo to various ships throughout the harbor.

At 0920, the old gunboat *Sacramento* sent a motor launch across the channel from 1010 dock to help save the men trapped alive aboard *Oklahoma* in compartments rapidly filling with water. The gunboat moved twenty-seven men off the ship to safety, but rescue operations were just beginning. With their acetylene torches flared and sweating, oil- and smoke-blackened men worked desperately through the night to free their suffocating comrades. The last of thirty-two survivors would not see daylight until late the next afternoon, some thirty-six hours after *Oklahoma* had rolled over. Four hundred and forty-eight men died aboard *Oklahoma* at Pearl Harbor.

(Above, left) A jumbled mass of wreckage was all that remained of the destroyers Downes *and* Cassin *after the attack on Pearl Harbor. (Above) Another destroyer,* Shaw, *illuminates the skies over Pearl Harbor as its forward ammunition magazine explodes.*

Moored in 1010 dock, about a quarter-mile south of drydock one, the light cruiser *Honolulu* was attempting to get under way at 0925 when another group of dive-bombers bored in. Three bombs struck just forward of the light cruiser *St. Louis*, moored between *Honolulu* and the heavy cruiser *San Francisco*. Then a fourth bomb landed on the pier, about fifteen feet from *Honolulu*'s side. The blasts opened the cruiser's oil tanks to the sea and caused considerable flooding. *Honolulu* lost steam—and thus electrical power for lighting and electrically operated guns—and was condemned to remain in place. Her crew derived some solace, however, by shooting down one of the attackers.

Across the pier from the *San Francisco*, much the same fate befell the heavy cruiser *New Orleans*, when something severed its power line to the dock. Despite disabled ammunition hoists, *New Orleans* was still a fighting ship. In the dark below decks, crew members formed a human conveyer belt to pass powder and shells topside to keep its guns firing.

While they worked, Chaplain Howell Forgy brought them apples and oranges and encouraging words. He apologized to the gun crews for being unable to hold church services that Sunday. Instead, he told them to "praise the Lord and pass the ammunition." His words moved the men deeply and later inspired one of the most enduring and soul-stirring songs of World War II.

Crew members of New Orleans *will long remember Chaplain Howell Forgy (pictured) for his inspirational words during the attack. (Below) Sailors stand atop the hull of the overturned* Oklahoma, *on which 448 men perished.*

One Hour and Fifty Minutes

At 0944, the garbage barge *YG 17* and its stern crew braved fire and exploding shells to tie up alongside *West Virginia* and pour streams of waters on the fires yet ablaze on the battleship. A minute later, the skies cleared. It was then 0945—one hour and fifty minutes after the first bomb had struck Ford Island.

The Japanese attack on Pearl Harbor had ended—and America's greatest war had begun.

Disregarding their own safety, sailors attempt to extinguish fires aboard the blazing West Virginia.

EPILOGUE

Rumors, Ruins, and Remembrance

Fuchida's first wave arrived back at *Kido Butai* at 1000. Fuchida himself, who had remained behind to direct the second wave, followed at 1200. Every Japanese aircraft capable of returning had done so by 1214. At 1315, Admiral Chuichi Nagumo ordered the withdrawal of *Kido Butai*. Nagumo's striking force, again under strict radio silence, turned homeward.

Amid the chaos and confusion that prevailed on Oahu that morning, the U.S. Navy managed only once to discover the slightest clue as to the location of the Japanese fleet. When Nagumo broke radio silence to report to Tokyo at 1030, a navy radio technician intercepted the Japanese transmission signal. This enabled the technician to fix the signal at either a source bearing of 357 degrees, almost due north, or from the directly opposite bearing of 3 degrees. Extending its run of bad luck, the navy mistakenly interpreted the signal as originating from south of Oahu. As a result of this error, American search activities were concentrated in the south, while *Kido Butai* slipped away to the north.

Rumors

Immediately after the last Japanese airplane cleared Oahu's skies, a wave of rumors surged across the island. The myth of a "third attack" pervaded both the military and civilian populations. In a report to Chief of Staff Marshall, General Short himself declared, "I would say at that time a definite attack was at 11:30." Marshall passed the report along to President Roosevelt.

My Country?

The Territorial Guard, the Hawaiian equivalent to the mainland's National Guard—was activated on December 7 and assigned to guard key public buildings and other important installations. Second-generation Japanese—*nisei*—represented a large segment of the Guard, which primarily consisted of Reserve Officers Training Corps (ROTC) students from the University of Hawaii and Honolulu high schools.

Nisei members of the guard felt a special sense of pride and privilege at the chance to serve their country under the tragic circumstances. One *nisei* guard member recalled, "We had not only the immediate emergency to spur us on, but the deeper purpose of establishing, once and for all, confidence in the actions of the Nisei in Hawaii as well."

But in the face of imminent invasion and widespread rumors of Japanese spies and saboteurs, the military government disbanded the Territorial Guard on the following January 23. Considering the critical shortage of military personnel, it became clear that distrust of Japanese-Americans caused the dissolution. This provoked bitter resentment among *nisei* members, one of whom wrote:

> Never in my life did I feel so bitter, so disappointed and so hopeless as when the discharge papers were handed to us. How can one feel otherwise when he [exiles] from the country of his ancestors to which he was a subject by legal formality and tries to become 100% American and further voluntarily enlists in the Army in time of war to sacrifice himself and is told "You are not wanted." What country can I call "Mea Patria" ["My Country"]? I am no longer a subject of Japan. I am an American citizen, but am treated as a despicable outcast.

"Enemy Air Attack resumed 11:00 a.m., much less intense than former attack." Vivid accounts of the third attack appeared in rich detail in official army and navy reports, newspaper articles, and government memoranda. A third attack never happened.

German Stuka dive-bombers were spotted, as were Japanese paratroopers. The threat of an imminent Japanese invasion spread across Oahu like pollen in a windstorm. Storekeeper Third Class Jack Rogo wrote that "rumors were coming in fast and furious. 'They are landing on Oahu.' 'They are landing north of us.' We couldn't tell truth from fiction, but we were going to be ready." Rogo traded his .45 pistol for a .30-caliber Springfield rifle.

Invasion rumors persisted for many days after the attack and would, in fact, become part of Hawaii's everyday life until the great American naval victory at Midway in June 1942. That victory curbed Japan's ability to launch an amphibious operation of that size.

Chief Boilermaker John Crawford, off the repair ship *Vestal*, might have welcomed another crack at the Japanese that morning, after seeing Americans being "hauled out of the water like fish" and moved to Aiea Dock. He recalled that

> most of them were all wrapped up by the time they got ashore and no one knew who they were. They were stretched out there on Aiea Dock like so many sacks of wheat. If I could have gotten my hands on any one of those Japanese, I would have crushed him like an insect.

Thousands of other Americans at Pearl Harbor shared his feelings. But the Japanese would not return to Oahu that day . . . or any other.

Ruins

Even today, more than a half-century after the event, more than a few military analysts and historians remain critical of Admiral Nagumo's failure to launch a second attack on Pearl Harbor when American defenses were in a state of total disarray. Many of those who took part in the first attack, including the attack leader Mitsuo Fuchida, favored a second attack. But Nagumo opted to stay strictly within the limits of his two mission objectives: to render the U.S. Pacific Fleet ineffective for at least six months and to return *Kido Butai* to Japan intact. He accomplished those objectives beyond his wildest imaginings.

In 110 minutes, the Japanese attackers had sunk five battleships—*Arizona, California, Nevada, Oklahoma,* and *West Virginia*—and seriously damaged three more—*Pennsylvania, Maryland,* and *Tennessee.* Also severely damaged were the light cruisers *Helena, Honolulu,* and *Raleigh* and the destroyers *Cassin, Downes, Helm,* and *Shaw.* The target ship *Utah* capsized, as did the minelayer *Oglala.* Four additional auxiliary vessels were badly hit: the seaplane tender *Curtiss,* the tug *Sotoyomo,* the repair ship *Vestal,* and the floating drydock two. The number of American vessels sunk or crippled totaled twenty-one.

American aircraft losses, both on the ground and in the air, numbered 165 planes.

Assessed damage to Oahu's military installations ran well into the millions of dollars, with damages to the Pearl Harbor navy yard alone estimated at $40 million (although that figure was probably inflated). But the greatest hurt came in American lives.

The total U.S. casualty figures recognized by most American authorities are 2,403 dead and 1,178 wounded. The majority of navy and marine deaths occurred on *Arizona,* while most army casualties were distributed among air corps personnel at Hickam and Wheeler Fields.

Despite the widespread suffering and ruin left at Pearl Harbor by Japanese guns, bombs, and torpedoes, the situation could have been worse. For instance, the navy yard's oil reserves—a

In the aftermath of the attack on Pearl Harbor, military installations across Oahu were left in ruins. Damages were estimated in the millions, forcing the United States to rebuild its once powerful fleet.

target even more vital than the warships—were not harmed. As Admiral Kimmel pointed out:

> If they had destroyed the oil which was all above ground at that time . . . it would have forced the withdrawal of the fleet to the [U.S. mainland] coast because there wasn't any oil anywhere else out there to keep the fleet operating.

Even so, the Japanese attackers had all but demolished America's defensive stronghold in the Pacific. And they had done so at the amazingly low cost of twenty-nine aircraft—three fighters, one dive-bomber, and five torpedo planes in the first wave; six fighters and fourteen dive-bombers in the second.

After receiving permission from Congress (above, right), President Roosevelt signs the declaration of war against Japan on December 8, 1941.

Remembrance

Admiral Isoroku Yamamoto had demonstrated the enormous destructive force of a carrier-launched attack. Moreover, he had proved the carrier's superiority over the more conventional battleship. He had achieved a great but tainted victory. The U.S. Navy was down but not out and would meet Yamamoto again in six months at Midway.

In the interim, Americans would regroup and together set their minds to the task of winning an unwanted war. And they would long remember what happened at Pearl Harbor.

Shortly after noon on December 8, 1941, President Franklin D. Roosevelt addressed the Congress of the United States. In a solemn voice, he began, "Yesterday, December 7, 1941—a date that will live in infamy—the United States of America was suddenly and deliberately attacked by the naval and air forces of Japan."

The president pointed out that the attack had been planned and carried out while Japan pretended to negotiate for peace. He assessed American losses and asked for American determination and resolve, while expressing confidence in American armed forces.

In conclusion, President Roosevelt said, "I ask that the Congress declare that since the unprovoked and dastardly attack by Japan on Sunday, December 7, 1941, a state of war has existed between the United States and the Japanese Empire." With but one dissenting voice in the House of Representatives, Congress did.

Appendix: Aircraft Directory

A6M: The Mitsubishi A6M "Zero" single-seat fighter and fighter-bomber was developed for the Japanese naval air force and first flown in April 1939. It was the only fighter plane used by the Japanese at Pearl Harbor and was superior to all American fighter planes at that time. It had a maximum speed of 332 miles per hour. Armament consisted of two 20-millimeter cannons and two 13.2-millimeter machine guns. The Zero was used throughout the Pacific theater and became one of the most famous and most produced fighter planes of World War II. Evidence of the Zero's versatility could be seen in some models that were equipped with floats. Affixing pontoons to the fighter enabled the Zeros to be catapulted from the cruisers *Tone* and *Chikuma* and used to provide advance reconnaissance for Pearl Harbor attack waves.

A-20: The Douglas A-20 "Havoc" was a twin-engine attack bomber first flown in 1938. It was armed with nine .50-caliber machine guns and carried a two-thousand-pound bomb load. Its maximum speed was 332 miles per hour.

B5N: Used primarily as a torpedo bomber, the Nakajima B5N "Kate" also served as a dive-bomber. The Kate carried a crew of two or three at speeds up to 225 miles per hour. It was armed with two 7.7-millimeter machine guns, one of which was mounted in the rear cockpit.

B-17: First flown in 1935, the Boeing B-17 "Flying Fortress" was a four-engine heavy bomber that was produced in several versions during World War II. Crew sizes varied from six to ten. The B-17 flew at speeds up to three hundred miles per hour. Its armament consisted of thirteen .50-caliber machine guns, and it carried a six-thousand-pound bomb load.

B-18: Developed in 1936, the Douglas B-18 "Bolo" was a twin-engine medium bomber that saw very limited service. Only 217 were made. Later versions equipped with radar were used for submarine patrols.

D3A: An awkward-looking, single-engine dive-bomber, with fixed landing gear, the Aichi "Val" became Japan's most effective bomber, sinking more Allied tonnage than any other bomber during the war. The Val was used most effectively at Pearl Harbor. It carried a crew of two at a top speed of 240 miles per hour. Armed with three 7.7-millimeter machine guns, it had an 813-pound bomb load capacity.

P-26: The Army Air Corps's first monoplane, all-metal production fighter, the Boeing P-26 "Peashooter" first flew in 1932 and entered service the following year. Obsolete before the start of World War II, the P-26 was slow (maximum speed of 234 miles per hour) and under-armed (two .30-caliber machine guns, or one .30-caliber and one .50-caliber machine gun).

P-36: Developed for the Army Air Corps, the Curtiss "Hawk" was first flown in April 1936. The Hawk, a single-engine, single-seat fighter, was already outdated at the time of Pearl Harbor. It flew at speeds of 325 miles per hour and was armed with one .50-caliber and three .30-caliber machine guns.

P-40: A reworked P-36, the Curtiss P-40 "Tomahawk" represented the only relatively modern fighter in service when the Japanese struck Pearl Harbor. It had a top speed of 352 miles per hour and was armed with two .30-caliber and two .50-caliber machine guns. The Flying Tigers flew the Tomahawk with great success against the Zero in China during the first six months of the war.

SBD: Although conceived in 1938, the Douglas SBD "Dauntless" achieved distinction as the best dive-bomber designed and built by the American aircraft industry during World War II. The Dauntless carried a crew of two, flew at a maximum speed of 250 miles per hour, and had a maximum range of 1,345 miles. Armed with two .30-caliber and two .50-caliber machine guns, it could carry a twelve-hundred-pound bomb load.

Glossary

aft: Rear.

Atarimashita!: "It struck!"

Axis: Military alliance formed by Germany, Italy, and Japan during World War II.

Banzai!: Japanese battle cry; original meaning, "May you live forever!"

battlewagon: Battleship.

bearing: A compass direction.

bow: The extreme forward part of a ship.

Bushido: The code of conduct of the *samurai* of Japan, which embraces the virtues of courage, self-discipline, courtesy, gentleness, and honoring one's word.

China Incident: Japanese invasion of China; eight-year war between China and Japan commencing in 1937.

CinCUS: Commander in chief of the U.S. fleet.

CinPAC: Commander in chief of the U.S. Pacific Fleet.

CNO: Chief of naval operations.

conning tower: A raised structure on a submarine containing the periscope.

cryptanalyst: An expert in decoding coded messages; code breaker.

depth charge: An explosive device used against submarines, designed to detonate at a preset depth.

dive-bombing: a steep-dive (hell-diving) bombing approach.

embargo: A government order prohibiting the departure of commercial ships or goods from its ports.

emperor: Ruler of an empire, as Emperor Hirohito of Japan.

envoy: A person delegated to represent one government in its dealings with another.

fantail: Aft end of a ship.

flagship: A ship that carries an admiral and carries his flag.

flattop: Aircraft carrier.

forward: At or toward the front of a ship.

great all-out battle strategy: Japanese naval strategy based on luring the U.S. fleet—after first being weakened by Japanese submarine activity—into Japanese home waters for a massive, decisive sea battle for control of the Pacific Ocean.

greater East Asia coprosperity sphere: Japanese policy that called for the recognition of economic and political ties between Japan and several Southeast Asian nations.

grid location: A geographical location defined by an intersection of latitude and longitude lines on a map.

hachimaki: Headband worn by Japanese pilots.

hara-kiri: A ritual suicide by cutting out one's bowels, formerly practiced by Japanese officers when in disgrace or under sentence of death; also *hari-kiri*.

high-level bombing: A high-altitude, level-flight approach to deliver bombs on target.

Hisso: Certain Victory (message marked on *hachimaki*).

hull: The basic frame of a ship or aircraft.

intercept: Head off.

Kido Butai: Carrier striking force.

Kodo-Ha: The way of the emperor; a Japanese political movement that supported a totalitarian state controlled by the army.

League of Nations: Formed after World War I to prevent war and promote international cooperation; at one time the league had about sixty members.

logistics: Organization of military supplies and services.

MAG: Marine air group.

magazine: A store for arms and ammunition; a holder in or on a gun for cartridges to be fed into the gun chamber.

Manchukuo: Japanese puppet state formed after Japanese invasion of Manchuria in 1931.

Midway: Atoll located thirteen hundred miles west-northwest of Hawaii; site of great American naval victory over the Japanese on June 4–7, 1942.

militarist: One who advocates a policy of aggressive military preparedness.

modus vivendi: A workable arrangement or compromise.

ordnance: Military weapons, and their equipment and ammunition.

Operation Hawaii: Japanese code name for the Pearl Harbor attack; later changed to Operation Z.

Operation Z: Japanese code name for the Pearl Harbor attack; earlier called Operation Hawaii.

Pearl Harbor: U.S. naval installation at Oahu, Hawaii; headquarters of the U.S. Pacific Fleet.

perimeter: A line or strip bounding or protecting an area; outer limits.

port: Left side (of a ship).

radar: A system for detecting the presence, position, or movement, etc., of objects by sending out short radio waves that are reflected by the objects.

reconnaissance: A preliminary search to gain information, especially for military purposes.

rendezvous: A meeting place.

Rengo Kantai: Combined Fleet.

sabotage: Willful damaging of materials or property or disruption of work by dissatisfied workers or hostile agents.

samurai: A military retainer of a Japanese *daimyo* practicing the warrior code of *Bushido;* the warrior upper class of Japan.

Senken Butai: Advance force.

shogun: One of a line of military governors ruling Japan until the revolution of 1867–1868.

Sino-: Chinese.

starboard: Right side (of a ship).

strategy: The plan for the entire operation of a war or campaign.

tactics: The art of placing or maneuvering forces skillfully in a battle.

torpedo bombing: A bombing technique that employs an extremely low and slow approach to deliver a torpedo on target.

"Tora! Tora! Tora!": "Tiger! Tiger! Tiger!" (message sent to Admiral Nagumo by Commander Fuchida to signify that the attack on Pearl Harbor was indeed a surprise).

totsugekiseyo: "Charge!" (*"To, To, To!"*)

Treaty of Kanagawa: Treaty opening Japan to Western trade, signed by American commodore Matthew C. Perry and Japanese shogun Iyeyoshi in 1854.

Tripartite Pact: Formal agreement that established a military alliance between Germany, Italy, and Japan during World War II; the three nations became known as the Axis powers, or the Axis.

Washington Naval Conference: Disarmament conference convened in Washington, D.C., during 1921–1922, which limited Japanese warship construction to three tons for each five tons built by the United States and Great Britain; that is, a 5-5-3 tonnage ratio.

X day: December 7, 1941 (December 8 in Japan); the Japanese equivalent of D day; the date on which a military operation is set to begin.

For Further Reading

David Bergamini, *Japan's Imperial Conspiracy*. New York: Pocket Books, 1972. A massive, controversial book that indicts Emperor Hirohito as a war criminal, written by a Rhodes scholar and former editor of *Life* magazine.

Robert J. Casey, *Torpedo Junction: With the Pacific Fleet from Pearl Harbor to Midway*. New York: Bobbs-Merrill, 1942. A personal reminiscence of the first six months of the naval war in the Pacific by a noted war correspondent and author.

Winston S. Churchill, *The Grand Alliance*. Boston: Houghton Mifflin, 1950. Sir Winston's marvelous recounting of World War II from January 1941 through January 1942, featuring America's entry into the war.

Eugene Lyon, "America on the Brink of War," in *The Reader's Digest Illustrated Story of World War II*. Pleasantville, NY: The Reader's Digest Association, 1969. A glimpse of one of the wildest, most colorful periods in American history.

Masatake Okumiya and Jiro Horikoshi with Martin Caidin, *Zero!* New York: Ballantine Books, 1956. The story of Japan's air war in the Pacific by a Japanese commander of many of its sea-air battles and the designer of a famous fighter plane; includes insightful text on the Japanese view of the Pearl Harbor attack.

Zenji Orita with Joseph D. Harrington, *I-Boat Captain*. Canoga Park, CA: Major Books, 1978. A Japanese submarine captain writes about the undersea war in the Pacific, including a periscoped view of the submariner's role in the attack on Pearl Harbor.

Saburo Sakai with Martin Caidin and Fred Saito, *Samurai!* New York: Ballantine Books, 1957. A personal account of Japan's air war in the Pacific, written by the greatest Japanese fighter pilot to survive the war; includes an interesting account of Japan's December 8 attack on the Philippines, executed simultaneously with the attack on Pearl Harbor.

William L. Shirer, *The Rise and Fall of the Third Reich: A History of Nazi Germany*. New York: Simon and Schuster, 1959. A history of Hitler's Reich by a highly regarded foreign correspondent and historian. Contains valuable insight into the German-Italian-Japanese Axis during World War II.

Donald J. Young, *December 1941: America's First 25 Days at War*. Missoula, MT: Pictorial Histories Publishing, 1992. A fascinating, illustrated account of America's first twenty-five days at war in World War II.

Works Consulted

Henry Berry, *"This Is No Drill!"* New York: Berkley Books, 1992. An oral history told through the personal accounts of survivors of the attack on Pearl Harbor.

Blake Clark, "Remember Pearl Harbor!" in *Reader's Digest Illustrated Story of World War II.* Pleasantville, NY: The Reader's Digest Association, 1969. A professor of history at the University of Hawaii describes what it was like on that Sunday morning when bombs began to fall on the Hawaiian island of Oahu.

Henry C. Clausen and Bruce Lee, *Pearl Harbor: Final Judgement.* New York: Crown Publishers, 1992. Clausen, a former special investigator for Secretary of War Henry L. Stimson, and Lee, an esteemed editor of military manuscripts, have written a book that provides accurate and irrefutable answers to all the "unanswered" questions surrounding Pearl Harbor.

R. Ernest Dupuy and Trevor N. Dupuy, *The Encyclopedia of Military History.* New York: Harper & Row, 1977. A monumental work on warfare by two noted historians; includes a keen analysis of events occurring before, during, and immediately after Japan's attack on Pearl Harbor.

Mitsuo Fuchida, "I Led the Attack on Pearl Harbor," in *Reader's Digest Illustrated Story of World War II.* Pleasantville, NY: The Reader's Digest Association, 1969. A firsthand account of the Japanese air attack on Pearl Harbor written by the pilot who led it.

Donald M. Goldstein and Katherine V. Dillon, editors, *The Pearl Harbor Papers: Inside the Japanese Plans.* New York: Brassey's, 1993. An outstanding book that reveals original Japanese documents on Operation Hawaii, including secret plans, battle group histories, and the intimate letters and diaries of the key Japanese naval officers who planned, organized, and executed the attack on Pearl Harbor.

Edward Jablonski, *Airwar.* Vol. I. Garden City, NY: Doubleday, 1971. A history of aerial warfare during World War II; contains an excellent chapter on the Pearl Harbor attack, including some fine photographs of the action.

Walter Lord, *Day of Infamy.* New York: Bantam Books, 1991. A gripping, vivid re-creation of Japan's infamous sneak attack on Pearl Harbor on Sunday, December 7, 1941.

Samuel Eliot Morison, "How and Why Japan Prepared for World War," in *Reader's Digest Illustrated Story of World War II.* Pleasantville, NY: The Reader's Digest Association, 1969. A famous naval historian reviews how Japan planned and prepared for war during the 1930s.

Iain Parsons, editor, *The Encyclopedia of Air Warfare.* New York: Thomas Y. Crowell, 1974. A comprehensive study of aerial warfare, from the beginning of powered flight until 1974. The book includes a brief but excellent account of the Pearl Harbor attack.

Gordon W. Prange with Donald L. Goldstein and Katherine V. Dillon, *At Dawn We Slept: The Untold Story of Pearl Harbor.* New York: McGraw-Hill, 1981. An authentic, absorbing account of Pearl Harbor from both the U.S. and the Japanese points of view; the masterwork on the event, its causes, and its aftermath by an historian who spent thirty-seven years preparing his book.

———, *December 7, 1941: The Day the Japanese Attacked Pearl Harbor.* New York: McGraw-Hill, 1988. A classic work that concentrates on the events that occurred immediately before, during, and after the Japanese attack on that long-remembered day.

———, *Pearl Harbor: The Verdict of History*. New York: Penguin Books, 1991. An exacting analysis of the underlying causes of Pearl Harbor.

Clark G. Reynolds and the editors of Time-Life Books, *The Carrier War*. Alexandria, VA: Time-Life Books, 1982. A well-written and beautifully illustrated history of carrier warfare in World War II, including an excellent chapter on the Japanese attack on Pearl Harbor.

Michael Slackman, *Target: Pearl Harbor*. Honolulu: University of Hawaii Press, 1990. A fresh overview of the Pearl Harbor attack that uses contemporary documents and interviews with survivors to re-create the event and to examine its causes and the reasons for America's unpreparedness.

Louis L. Snyder, "Why the Sneak Attack Succeeded," in *Reader's Digest Illustrated Story of World War II*. Pleasantville, NY: The Reader's Digest Association, 1969. An examination of the deceptive methods used by the Japanese to achieve surprise at Pearl Harbor and of the elements of chance that assisted them.

John Toland, *But Not in Shame*. New York: The New American Library of World Literature, 1961. A remarkable history of the crucial first six months of the Pacific war, including a vivid depiction of the Pearl Harbor attack.

———, *Infamy: Pearl Harbor and Its Aftermath*. New York: Berkley Books, 1983. The noted historian's shocking and revealing account of Pearl Harbor's aftermath and the attempts to find scapegoats and cover up facts that might affix blame in high places.

———, *The Rising Sun*. New York: Random House, 1970. A narrative history of modern Japan from the invasion of Manchuria and China to the atom bomb; includes a fine account of the Pearl Harbor attack and the events leading up to it.

Stephen Bowers Young, *Trapped at Pearl Harbor: Escape from Battleship* Oklahoma. New York: Dell Publishing, 1991. The tragic tale of the more than four hundred men who died aboard *Oklahoma* and of a handful of men who escaped entrapment aboard the capsized vessel, written by one of the survivors.

Index

Picture Credits

Cover photo: Library of Congress

AP/Wide World Photos, 31 (top), 75

Archive Photos, 20, 35, 67 (bottom), 73 (top)

Franklin D. Roosevelt Library, 63

Library of Congress, 13 (both), 14, 41, 43, 47, 57 (top), 59, 64, 67 (top), 69 (top), 70, 73 (bottom), 76 (top), 78 (top), 82, 88, 89 (top), 90, 93 (bottom), 95, 99 (top)

National Archives, 10, 12 (top), 16, 21 (both), 26, 32, 33, 39, 42, 44, 49, 51 (both), 55 (middle), 57 (bottom), 60, 65, 69 (bottom), 72 (bottom), 76 (bottom), 78 (bottom), 85, 86, 93 (top), 94 (bottom), 99 (bottom), 100 (both)

UPI/Bettmann, 12 (bottom), 23, 28, 31 (bottom), 55 (top and bottom), 72 (top), 79, 80, 83 (both), 89 (bottom), 94 (top)

About the Author

Earle Rice Jr. has authored eleven previous books for young adults, including fast-action fiction and adaptations of *Dracula* and *All Quiet on the Western Front*. Mr. Rice has written several books for Lucent, including *The Cuban Revolution, The Battle of Britain,* and *The Battle of Midway*. He has also written numerous articles, short stories, and technical documents.

After serving nine years with the U.S. Marine Corps, Mr. Rice attended San Jose City College and Foothill College on the San Francisco peninsula.

Mr. Rice is a former aerospace design engineer who now devotes full time to his writing. He lives in Julian, California, with his wife, daughter, granddaughter, two cats, and a dog.